Brush, Sponge, Stamp

A creative guide to painting beautiful patterns on everyday surfaces.

Artwork by Paula DeSimone
Text by Pat Stewart

Quarry Books
Rockport Publishers, Gloucester, Massachusetts
North Light Books,
Cincinnati, Ohio

First published in the United States of America by:
Quarry Books, an imprint of
Rockport Publishers, Inc.
33 Commercial Street
Gloucester, Massachusetts 01930-5089
Telephone: (508) 282-9590
Fax: (508) 283-2742

Distributed to the book trade and art trade in the United States by:
North Light Books, an imprint of
F & W Publications
1507 Dana Avenue
Cincinnati, Ohio 45207
Telephone: (800) 289-0963

Other distribution by:
Rockport Publishers, Inc.
Gloucester, Massachusetts 01930-5089

ISBN 1-56496-353-5

10 9 8 7 6 5 4 3 2 1

Design: Beth Santos Design
Cover Photography: Martin Berinstein

Printed in Hong Kong

The rendering of a Peruvian weaving in Peruvian Patterns; the Glowing Beads pattern; the origami boxes, pins, and earrings in the gifts section; and the quilt in Crazy Quilt, were created by Pat Stewart. The writing paper, business card, barrette, and notebook in Creative Uses were designed by Heather Yale, using Paula DeSimone's artwork. "After Rain" by Huang Xuanzhi was borrowed from the collection of Pat and Henry Stewart.

Photography by Martin Berinstein.

COLOUR SHAPER® is a registered trademark of Forsline & Starr International Ltd.

ACKNOWLEDGMENTS

Many people helped with the preparation of this book. We are especially grateful to Lori Hedler of Devonia Antiques for Dining, 43 Charles Street, Boston, Massachusetts, for giving us the run of the shop and letting us borrow the china shown in Color Inspirations; Glen Baxter and Akihiko Shimizu of Boston, who provided translation and research help on the Chinese painter Huang Xuanzhi; Shirley Miller of Loew-Cornell, who provided us with brushes; Barbara Carson of Delta Technical Coating, who provided paints, and Susanna Starr and Ladd Forsline of Forsline & Starr, who provided Colour Shapers; and the library of the Museum of Fine Arts, Boston, for research assistance. We also owe the warmest gratitude to Martin Berinstein, our photographer, whose good nature and professionalism made photo shoots fun.

We could not have managed our professional and personal responsibilities during the writing of this book without help from our husbands. Paula DeSimone thanks her husband Joseph for his support and understanding; Pat Stewart thanks her husband Henry for his patience and encouragement. We dedicate this book to these wonderful men.

CONTENTS

INTRODUCTION
DECORATIVE PAINTING AS A CREATIVE PROCESS

The term *decorative painting* conjures up a range of images: early humans recording the results of a mammoth hunt on the cave wall; artisans in French studios applying elaborate gilding to fine furniture; or Edwardian ladies painting roses on tole trays. Decorative painting is all of this and more.

We define decorative painting broadly as applying painted textures, forms, and patterns to useful surfaces. We also believe the best decorative painting is an art, not a craft. The contemporary decorative painter is motivated by many of the same desires that motivated these early decorative painters:

- to create unique, expressive living environments

- to earn appreciation and (perhaps some income) for one's talent

- to spend discretionary time in a way that combines utility with personal expression.

The contemporary decorative painter enjoys many advantages, including the fine examples of decorative art left by earlier painters, the ready availability of new and improved materials, and a society that appreciates art and innovation. Today, creativity and individual artistic expression are more valued than ever before.

Opportunities to learn and practice decorative painting abound. Every day, aspiring decorative artists join classes at museums, art schools, and adult education centers, in record numbers. This book may serve as a text or supplement to such courses or as a guide to independent work.

In response to growing interest in decorative painting, the number of fine books on the subject is increasing. (You will find a list of some useful resources in the back of this book.) Most of these, however, focus on traditional subjects and techniques—roses and fruit, tassels and ribbons, fancy brushwork, and various common surface textures, such as sponging and glazing. This book represents a departure from tradition. It provides an opportunity to study, learn, apply, and combine simple techniques to create contemporary patterns and textures that look rich and complex. While many of the patterns shown rely on simple brushwork, others employ other techniques—for instance, stamping with unusual tools, such as bubble wrap and rug liner.

How would you set about becoming a decorative artist? Or, if you already enjoy decorative painting, how can you add a contemporary complement to your portfolio of traditional skills? Part of the answer lies in technique. You will discover many novel but easy-to-replicate techniques in each section. But the key to artistry is creativity. With that in mind, we focus on the creative process that an artist follows in determining not only what to paint, but how to select among many decorative options and how to combine several techniques to create unique painted surfaces.

The creative process comes alive through a dozen projects that show not only what the artist did, but how the artist thought through the process and what might have been done had creative inspiration moved in another direction. Illustrations show many sources of inspiration from museum collections, books, historical artifacts, and nature. In addition, photographs of the how-to projects clearly depict each step in the execution of these particular works of useful art.

The components of the creative process for decorative painters include:

🌀 **Identifying and securing objects or surfaces**

🌀 **Finding and exploring sources of inspiration**

🌀 **Converting inspiration into design concepts**

🌀 **Exploring patterning through drawing your idea**

🌀 **Laying out your design**

🌀 **Preparing the surface**

🌀 **Transferring the design**

🌀 **Selecting and applying painting techniques**

🌀 **Producing a museum-quality finish**

The projects in this book follow the components of this creative process and, at the same time, provide step-by-step illustrations.

Sometimes, structure constrains; in other cases, structure liberates. We believe that aspiring artists benefit from understanding and working within a creative process that is suggestive, not prescriptive. Individual artists may expand, adapt, or improvise on a project at any stage of the process.

We also suggest alternatives for each project. A catalog of patterns and textures showcases many other possibilities for your consideration. You may be inspired to create your own unique interpretation or application. In the Creative Uses section, we demonstrate how to apply what you have learned to enhance surfaces in your home and to create pleasing, original gifts.

To further stimulate your creativity, a section on color inspirations is included at the end of the book. Each photograph of natural material, fine art, textile, or china is accompanied by a color palette drawn from the source of inspiration.

Who can enjoy decorative painting? Anyone. People who buy gifts in fancy boutiques can, instead, learn decorative painting as a way of creating unique, personalized presents for their friends and family. Busy professionals with hectic schedules can find time to learn to decorate a floor cloth or a piece of furniture, enriching their physical environment, as well as satisfying a creative urge. Retirees who never had a minute to themselves can now enjoy time spent in creative self-expression. People with a formal education in art can expand their talent and build their portfolio and repertoire, at the same time creating highly marketable expressions of their art.

What can you find to paint? Anything. Craft stores are stocked with standard items, such as boxes, trays, and plaques. But the alert artist will spot many less obvious opportunities to make the world more beautiful: that beat-up table in the basement; those old kitchen canisters that add nothing to the decor of your daily life; that interesting lamp or bowl on the flea market table that says, "Take me home and make me better." All of these objects and countless others can provide opportunities to try out the new ideas shown in this book or to create your own variations.

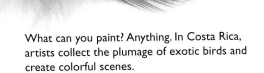

What can you paint? Anything. In Costa Rica, artists collect the plumage of exotic birds and create colorful scenes.

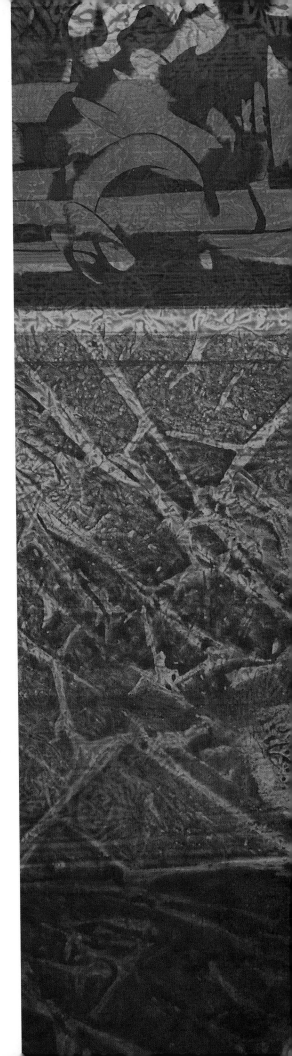

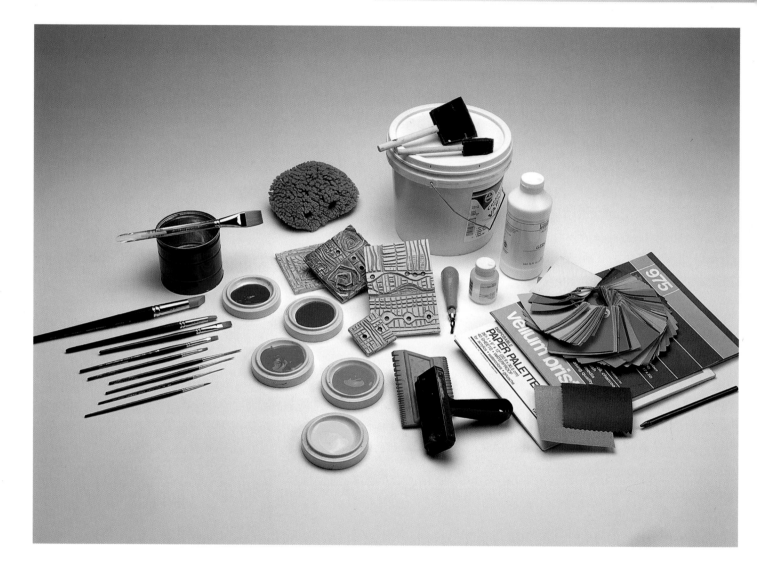

If you are not already equipped with basic
materials for decorative painting, the following
section will serve as a shopping list. Most art or
craft stores stock the materials described. Your
neighborhood hardware store carries some items,
such as sandpaper and sponge brushes. If you intend
to carry out one of the projects, you may prefer to use
only the specific materials listed for that project, to
limit your initial investment. Then as you move on to
another project, you can add to your supply of
materials.

BRUSHES

Synthetic brushes designed especially for decorative painting will help you achieve the lines and shapes shown throughout the book. Decorative painting brushes are shorter than those often used for oil painting. You will need five types of brushes. Other sizes may be specified in some projects, but you can usually substitute a brush one or two sizes smaller or larger.

- A #3 round brush produces clean, short strokes.

- Script liners in sizes 1, 4, and 6 will help you make flowing straight and curved lines of varying widths.

- Flat shaders in sizes 6, 8, 12, and 1" (2.5 cm) create stripes and curved shapes of varying widths depending on the size of the brush and the pressure applied. The 1" (2.5 cm) brush can also be used instead of the sponge brush for applying paints, colored glazes, and varnish.

- Colour Shapers are really "unbrushes." The hard rubber tip removes paint or glaze from the surface to let the underlying color or pattern show through. Sizes 6 and 12 Colour Shapers produce medium and wide strokes.

- Sponge brushes are used to apply primer, base coat, and varnish with a light touch. Sizes shown in the photo on page 10 are 1" (2.5 cm) and 3" (7.5 cm). As an alternative, you could also use soft bristle brushes for these tasks.

MEDIUMS

Decorative painting makes use of several mediums to color and coat surfaces and to change the properties of paint.

Water-based flow acrylic paint provides the color in decorative painting. This thick, pourable paint is about the consistency of very heavy cream. It is packaged in small bottles, usually with a spout to facilitate pouring small or larger amounts. Paint colors vary by manufacturer. You certainly need black, white, and the spectrum colors: red, orange, yellow, green, blue, and violet. You can mix other colors, tints, and shades from these basics, but you may wish to buy premixed colors that correspond to the colors used in our patterns or other colors that you like. Please note that the same color may be named differently by different manufacturers, therefore we have used descriptive names for colors. Your best guide for buying or mixing paint are the color samples themselves that appear at the beginning of the project.

Extender, or a related product, called blending medium, retards the drying time of paint without thinning the liquid property. Extender is used to allow more time for blending paint or for mixing glazes. Water can be used as an extender, but it does thin the liquid property of paint.

Water-based primer-sealer coats and fills unfinished wood to provide a foundation for subsequent coats of paint and varnish. If you paint on surfaces other than wood or similar surfaces, such as cardboard or papier-mâché, you will need other sealers. Metal should be prepared with metal primer; canvas or other fabric, with gesso.

Water-based varnish provides a base for paint and protects your work. Two coats of varnish seal in a layer of paint. You can add layers of paint or glaze on top of the varnish coats and then remove them back to the varnish coat if you are not satisfied with the results. Several layers of varnish build a smooth, protective finish for your work. Gloss varnish is used as a base for glazing and texturing, and provides an attractive, glossy finish. Use satin varnish for a less shiny finish. An eight-ounce bottle will serve the needs of most painters.

PAPERS

The papers used for decorative painting are the same as those used for other art and craft purposes.

Palette paper is a poly-coated paper, commonly sold in 9" x 12" (22.5 cm x 30 cm) pads of forty sheets or so. Palette paper allows paint to be mixed without soaking through. It can also be used to practice strokes or try out color combinations. Other effective paint-mixing surfaces include the polyfoam trays that meat is packaged on, paper plates, jar lids, and plastic palettes.

Bristol board, or vellum Bristol, is a two-ply pasted paper that provides a medium-tooth surface. Bristol board can be treated just like the surface you plan to paint. That means you can try out textures or patterns in a "safe" place. A 9" x 12" inch (22.5 cm x 30 cm) pad of twenty sheets is a useful size.

Sandpaper comes in different grades of abrasiveness. You will need an assortment, from medium to very fine, #150, #400, and #600. When you begin a project, #150 will smooth the rough edges to prepare for priming and painting; #400 smoothes between coats of paint and varnish steps, and #600 provides a fine polishing for wet sanding. You can also use new foam-backed superfine sanding pads for wet sanding.

You will find several other items helpful as you carry out the projects shown.

A water container is essential. No matter what you are painting, you will rinse your brush in water frequently to keep paint from drying in the brush and to change colors. Any container that holds about eight ounces of water, such as a glass, can, or yogurt container, will do.

Sponges are used to apply thinned paint to achieve a mottled effect. A natural sea sponge is best because of its irregular texture. Some artists buy a large sponge as shown and cut it into smaller pieces, depending on the effect they want to achieve. Cellulose kitchens sponges may be used as stamps.

Rubber printing blocks incised to form designs are used to stamp paint onto surfaces. Blocks are especially effective when a design is repeated to form a pattern.

A linoleum-cutting tool cuts away some of the rubber on the block to create a design.

Flexible rubber combs "rake" through paint or glaze to form areas of regularly spaced lines. Combing again at another angle produces cross-hatching or a woven effect. Polyfoam meat and vegetable trays from the supermarket can be cut with pinking shears to achieve a similar effect.

A roller spreads paints and glazes evenly onto a printing block or stamp.

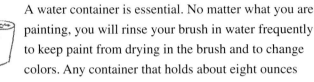A color ring will help you select pleasing color combinations. This example was created by the artist with hand-mixed colors, but you can also purchase a color ring at art supply stores.

A drawing pencil may be used to sketch out ideas in advance or to draw designs onto objects as guides for painting.

A quilter's pencil is ideal for sketching ideas on a painted surface because lines wash away easily.

Some everyday items commonly used in decorative painting include a sketch pad for noting ideas and experimenting with designs, paper towels, clear plastic wrap, bubble wrap, carpet liner, tracing or transfer paper, fine steel wool, and a hair dryer.

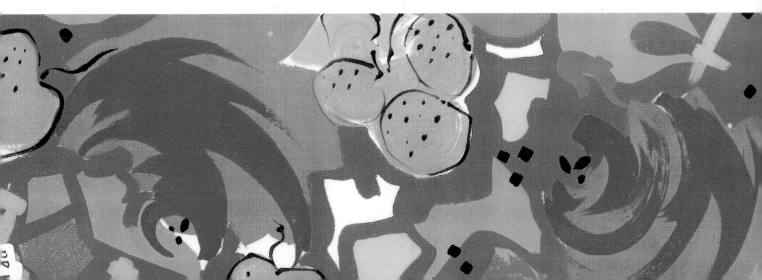

SURFACE PREPARATION AND FINISHING

If you want to produce fine, durable examples of decorative art, pay special attention to surface preparation. Nothing is more disappointing than noticing a rough spot in the middle of painting a pattern. Follow the procedure below whenever you decorate new wood surfaces. If you are working on an already painted surface in good condition, you may need only to clean and sand the old surface. If old paint or varnish is cracked or blistered, you will need to strip it down to bare wood, following the directions on your stripping product. Then follow the procedure for unfinished wood.

Fine artwork deserves a fine finish. When you are satisfied with your decorative application, you will want to ensure that it presents a smooth, museum-quality finish that is beautiful and will last with use. There is nothing worse than seeing a carefully wrought pattern fail to adhere or wear away with use.

SANDING

The first step in preparing your working surface is sanding it to a smooth finish. If the surface is rough, begin with a medium grade sandpaper (#150) and move progressively to fine (#400) and very fine (#600) papers. Whenever possible, sand with the grain of the wood. Run your fingers over the entire surface to make sure it is flawless. Minor imperfections can show through later finishes and spoil the final effect.

BASE COATING

The last major activity in preparing your surface is applying a base coat. Select a background color to suit your design. If you are working on a large piece, use a good-quality flat latex paint. It is less expensive and comes in larger containers than most acrylic paints. If the piece is small, using acrylic paints is fine. Sand lightly again. If the base coat does not cover evenly, apply another coat. When you are satisfied with the base coat, seal it by applying one or more coats of water-based varnish. Now the surface is ready for your design.

SEALING

Unfinished wood is porous and requires sealing to ensure that later applications of paint and varnish adhere properly. As a second step, apply one or two coats of a good quality primer-sealer. Sometimes, priming will raise the grain of the wood slightly. For this reason, sand again with #400 sandpaper between and after coats of sealer. Again, run your fingers over the surface to test for smoothness.

Because you will be applying many coats of paints and varnishes, you can speed up the drying process with an electric hair dryer. Just be careful not to blow dust or other debris into wet finishes. Also, hold the dryer 6" (15 cm) or more from the object. If you hold it too close, the heat may cause the paint to bubble.

MATERIALS FOR PREPARING AND FINISHING SURFACES

 2" (5 cm) bristle brush and a 1" to 2" (2.5 cm to 5 cm) sponge brush or sizes to suit your project

paint or varnish stripper, scraper and steel wool (if necessary for cracked paint or varnish)

 wood primer-sealer

paint for base coat; either flat latex or acrylic paint

 water-based gloss varnish; matte or satin varnish may also be used for some purposes

steel wool

 electric hair dryer (optional)

sandpaper #150, #400, and #600

VARNISHING

Careful varnishing enhances and protects your painting. Apply varnish in smooth, gentle strokes with a foam brush or a soft bristle brush. The foam brush is gentler than a bristle brush and assures that your paint will not be disturbed. But beware—the air pockets that provide the light touch can create tiny bubbles, so watch your results as you go. Also watch for drips and runs. Bubbles and drips can be removed easily when wet but are difficult to smooth away when dry. Be aware that varnish sets quickly, so remove imperfections right away but without overworking the surface. Brushing back and forth or going back after varnish has partially dried will produce an uneven surface. Apply three thin coats of varnish to safely seal your design.

Gloss varnish is best for most purposes. It enlivens colors and patterns and creates a slick base for other processes. Matte varnish creates a more muted look and a less durable finish. Outdoor varnish may be necessary for items that may be exposed to the weather, such as a sign, mailbox, or birdhouse.

WET SANDING

Wet sanding, the second step in surface finshing, smoothes any imperfections in your varnished surface and prepares it for subsequent layers of varnish. Wet a piece of #600 (superfine) sandpaper with mild soapy water and rub it gently over the surface. Remove any soap film with a damp cloth. Dry by gently patting with a clean cloth, paper towel, or by using a hair dryer. Dampness under the varnish may cause it to turn cloudy. When the surface is dry, varnish and wet sand again.

FINAL FINISHING

Repeat this cycle of varnishing and wet sanding four or five times or until the surface is perfectly smooth. Some very fine work may require up to twenty coats of varnish. Do not wet sand after the final coat of varnish. Instead, rub your work very gently with #000 steel wool. Wipe with a soft cloth to remove any residue. Admire the results.

BASIC BRUSHSTROKES

Although the projects and patterns shown in this book do not require fancy brushwork or elaborate technique, you will want to know how to execute a few basic strokes before you begin. If you have not painted before, you will feel more confident if you practice before undertaking a project. Use the brushes indicated and any colors you like. Practice the strokes illustrated on these pages on palette paper, using different-size brushes, pressing lightly on the brush and then bearing down. Save your practice sheets to maintain a record of your progress.

LINES

You can achieve a sophisticated look using even the simplest brushstrokes. The narrower lines are painted with a #4 script liner, the wider with a #6 script liner. For a less regular line, apply pressure as shown in the example farthest to the left in each set of strokes.

DOTS

You can paint dots in several ways. To paint small dots like the first four, use the tip of the #4 script liner. For another effect, try dipping the wrong end of the brush into the paint. Hold the brush end perpendicular to the surface and touch it with the tip to transfer the paint. A #6 script liner creates the first four larger dots. The fifth larger dot couldn't be easier. Just dip the tip of your finger into the paint and touch the surface lightly or firmly, depending on the size you want.

LINE PATTERNS

Lines of varying widths and lengths combine to form a
lively pattern. Note that the squares are really only
short, broad lines. You can create infinite variations on
this most elemental artistic form—the line.

LINE AND DOT PATTERNS

Combining simple lines and dots of different dimensions
and colors can create patterns that appear complex.
This pattern, used in the Mexican Motif painted box,
demonstrates the power of lines and dots. Even with these
simple lines and dots, be sure to practice on paper before you
apply paint to your surface.

CURVED LINES

If lines and dots can create rich patterns, imagine what curved lines can do! Curved lines require a little more practice, however. Use several sheets of palette paper to practice these strokes. When you have mastered them, you are ready to create all the patterns demonstrated in the pages that follow.

THE *S* STROKE

The *S* stroke is just what it seems—a slightly elongated rendering of the letter *S*. The top row shows the *S* stroke made (from left to right) with the #1 script liner, #2 script liner, the #8 flat shader, the #12 flat shader, and the #12 flat shader with pressure applied. The bottom row shows the inverted *S* strokes made with the same brushes. Although this stroke is just a backward *S*, it may seem awkward to produce at first.

THE SCROLL STROKE

The scroll stroke is an S stroke "with attitude." It requires more brush control than the S stroke but, with practice, you can easily master it. The illustration shows scroll strokes created with #1, #2, and #4 script liners.

LEAFY PATTERN

This attractive leafy pattern is deceptively simple. Each frond combines a curved line, which forms the stem, and a series of *S* and inverted *S* strokes.

SCROLL AND LEAF PATTERN

In this pattern, lavender scroll strokes form a backdrop for leaf shapes. Black and blue teardrop-shaped dots add detail to the pattern. The teardrops are made by painting a dot and pulling the brush a bit on one end before lifting it from the paper.

Objects

INSPIRATION *If you doubt that music can inspire graphic representation, think of the different images that come to mind when you hear Beethoven's "Fifth Symphony," the Beatles' "Sergeant Pepper's Lonely Hearts Club Band," and your national anthem. The lively, unrestrained spirit of improvisational jazz inspired this pattern. It is simultaneously hot and cool, simple and complex, free and controlled. The pattern, while pleasing as shown, invites experimentation and invention.*

Each color vibrates on its own, yet harmonizes with the others. The visual music occurs as the warm pink and light red contrast with the cooler red-violet and yellow-green. The brushstrokes themselves are like musical notes: Some are short, staccato rectangles; others are sustained spirals; while the stripes provide a base-line chord.

The pattern could be applied to almost any object.

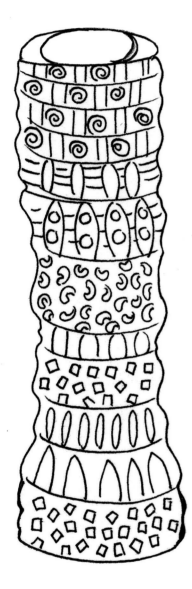

A large candlestick provides opportunities to apply colors and motifs in many combinations. Alone, it creates a stunning centerpiece for a round table. You might paint a pair for your mantle or sideboard. Or you can substitute simpler candlesticks. In any case, you might decide that the abundance of motifs is "too much" for your setting. If so, simplify the design by using basic stripes and one motif. The pattern could be applied to almost any object. If you choose another object, you might want to apply the patterns in the order shown or create your own harmony. If so, make a sketch of the object and experiment with alternatives.

A box, for example, might feature a different motif on each surface. Whatever object you choose, you may want to prepare a simple sketch, like the black-and-white design for the candlestick. Determine your design elements and prepare a sketch showing how you plan to arrange them on the object. If you're feeling spontaneous, wing it. Jazz master Duke Ellington said, "If it sounds good, it *is* good." We say, "If it *looks* good, it *is* good."

TOOLS AND MATERIALS

wooden candlestick, or other object large enough to accommodate this combination of colors and patterns

brushes: a broad brush, approximately 1" (2.5 cm); #1 and #4 script liners; #4, #6, and #12 flat shaders; and a 1" (2.5 cm) sponge brush (or brushes that achieve similar effects)

sealer-primer

water-based flow acrylic paints: black, pink, light red, red-violet, light red-violet, dark yellow-green

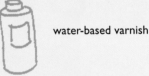

water-based varnish

sandpaper: medium grade (#150 or #400) and #600 superfine

extender or blending medium (for variation)

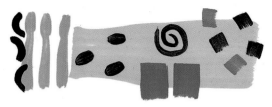

For this project, several simple brushstrokes form motifs.
These motifs, painted in bands, combine to build the overall design. Motifs include patterns of small squares, short and long stripes, and rounded cones made with flat shaders; spirals and small comma-like strokes executed with script liners; and dots. Make dots with a #6 script liner, with the wrong end of the brush, or with your fingertip.

1

Select your palette by painting color options adjacent to each other on a piece of palette paper. In this case, a pink base coat is overlaid with stripes and motifs in violet-red and black, combined with tints of red, red-violet, and a shade of yellow-green. Tints are achieved by adding white to a color; shades are achieved by adding black.

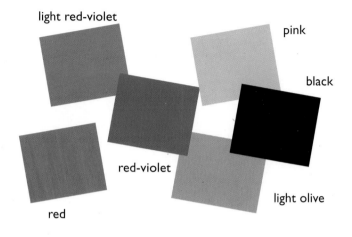

light red-violet

pink

black

red-violet

red

light olive

2

Prepare the candlestick for painting by sanding and sealing, described in Surface Preparation and Finishing. Then use a broad sponge or bristle brush to apply a pink base coat. Check for coverage. If necessary, apply a second coat. When the base coat is thoroughly dry, apply two coats of water-based varnish with the sponge brush.

3

With flat shaders, apply background stripes around the circumference of the candlestick in dark yellow-green, black, light red-violet, and light red. Varnish the stripes (or the entire piece, if easier).

4

Make renderings on Bristol board to clearly illustrate the various motifs, patterns, shapes, and strokes you can add to your piece. Using a #12 flat shader, apply the first motif variation, a checkerboard of red-violet rectangles, to the top portion of the candlestick. Note that each rectangle is just a short vertical stroke. Then, using a #6 flat shader, apply the second variation, a random pattern of smaller squares in red-violet, light red-violet, and black. Use the photo of the finished candlestick as a guide to applying the motifs. Or, if you feel creative, design your own arrangement.

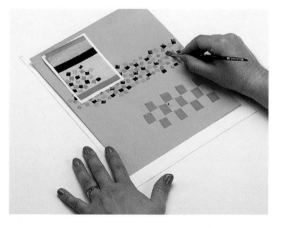

5 Using a #4 script liner, add a band of the second motif, a random pattern of short, black, curved strokes, to the middle section of the candlestick. Resist the tendency to paint the curved lines in rows. Rather, try to nest the curves into one another to achieve an integrated pattern. Note that the varnish you applied in previous steps allows you to wipe off any strokes you wish to do over.

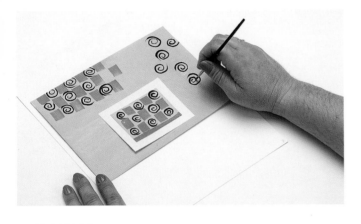

6 Use a #1 script liner to apply a third motif, a small black spiral, in the pink background spaces of the checkerboard, created in step 4. The spiral is nothing more than half of a scroll stroke.

7 Using a #4 script liner, add pink, black, and yellow-green dashes to the bands, as shown. Using the same brush, add dots to one or more of the bands of dashes. Press the brush down slightly to achieve larger dots or use your fingertip. On the remaining dark yellow-green bands, add stripes, dots, and dashes in patterns that copy the example or in patterns of your own. Then follow the steps in Surface Preparation and Finishing.

VARIATION: COOL JAZZ

What a difference a change in color makes! Base-painted a warm teal and embossed with gold stamps, the candlestick looks more subdued. Several small stamped designs, randomly applied, contribute spontaneity that is balanced by the formality of gilded details.

ART DECO FLORAL

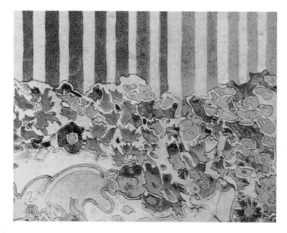

INSPIRATION *The rich color combinations and stylized shapes and patterns of the Art Deco period stunned the public in the 1920s. The sophisticated combination of simplified lines and complex patterns continue to intrigue us. As you leaf through reproductions of style books published in the early twentieth century, you may spot an arresting combination of colors, a compelling pattern detail, or even a sinuously curved shape. The example shown is a detail from a book illustration of the period. Note how the flowers are reduced to simple shapes and juxtaposed with other simple forms to create a unified pattern.*

The patterns carried out on the bowl embody the Art Deco influence. Brightly colored "roses" are nothing more than a combination of flat shapes in a pleasingly irregular arrangement. Likewise, simple, but visually interesting, black and white interlaced shapes form a complementary pattern on the outside surface of the bowl.

The focus is on the colorful surface inside the bowl.

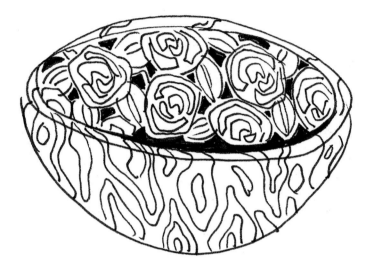

Both patterns are strong, but because the concave surface of the bowl uses color and the convex surface none, the focus is on the inside of this bowl. These patterns could be reversed for another effect. Note how the patterns from the bottom of the bowl wrap around and over the rim, integrating the two surfaces. These patterns would be as effective on any object with adjacent surfaces, such as a box, on which the lid could be one pattern and the sides another.

The bowl shown is about 12" (30 cm) in diameter; the flowers are 2" (5 cm) to 3" (7.5 cm) wide. On a larger bowl, these flowers might seem small. You could create a dramatic effect by painting one huge Georgia O'Keefe-like flower. To explore alternative scales and patterns, prepare black and white sketches as tests.

Now, what if the roses were magenta and pink or black and white and the black and white pattern was orange and pink? What if the roses were luscious green and purple grapes? Because few colors are used and the painting techniques are simple, you can create a bowl just like the one shown or paint any object featuring your own interpretation.

Remember the hours you spent with a coloring book and crayons, striving to stay within the lines?

Finally that skill will serve you well. Most of the painting for this project—the flowers and the black and white background—consists of creating shapes by coloring inside lines you have drawn on the bowl or object to be painted. Add definition by outlining those shapes in white. Leaf shapes can be painted in the same manner or can be formed using short *S* strokes. Form black dots with the #6 script liner, the wrong end of the brush, or your fingertip.

1 Select the colors for your project by painting possible combinations near one another on palette paper. Develop a pattern or, in this case, complementary patterns. Sketch the object and lay out your patterns so that you can see how the overall design works.

dark green   black   red

yellow-orange   red-orange

2 Sand and prime the bowl, as described in Surface Preparation and Finishing. Apply an even white base coat with the 1" (2.5 cm) brush. At each stage, wait for the paint or varnish to dry. Test for dryness by touching lightly in several places. Then, using your sketch as a guide, draw the pattern on the bowl. It might be possible to paint the design freehand; however, laying out the patterns on the object assures a balanced arrangement and gives you an opportunity to move shapes around.

DESIGN TIPS

Fabrics and wallpaper found in period houses can trigger design ideas. Carry a sketchbook when you travel so that you can record your ideas as you go. Check the library or used book sales for vintage books, many of which contain lovely borders and design details that are easy to adapt. Several style books focus on Art Deco patterns. For suggested titles, see the Resources section.

3 You have already selected your colors. Now, work out how you will use each color to implement your design. It is helpful to try this on paper first. If it is large enough, use a sketch you prepared in step 1. Otherwise, make a full-scale sketch to practice on. In this design, most of the center petal shapes are red and the outer petals are red-orange. The inner petal shapes are lined with white to set them off. The leaves are green, with white veins.

4 When you are satisfied with the painted design on paper, use a #6 flat shader to fill in the floral design you have sketched on the bowl itself. If your flowers are not perfect, don't worry. You can always tidy up the edges with white paint later. With the same brush, paint the leaves dark green. You can either fill in the leaf area or, if you are comfortable with your brush technique, form the leaves with short *S* strokes.

5 Add detail by painting black dots at the leaf edges with a #6 script liner. Once again, it is best to practice on paper to gain confidence and skill. Fill in any white areas between the flowers or at the bowl edges, where the pattern for the underside will wrap over. A #2 script liner will be best for edging the finer work. Use a #12 flat shader to paint larger areas.

6 On your full-scale practice sheet, fill in the yellow-orange background color to be sure it sets off the flowers and leaves to your satisfaction. Or you could experiment with other background colors. Then fill in the background on the bowl itself. Use the #2 script liner to outline in white any flower petals or leaves you may have missed. Notice that the original design wraps the outside pattern around to the inside, so be sure to leave white space if you wish to achieve the same effect.

7 After all the paint is dry, varnish the inside of the bowl to seal it. Then turn the bowl over and outline the black pattern with the #4 script liner. Touch up any parts of the pattern that require it. Varnish your entire bowl and complete the finishing process, as shown in Surface Preparation and Finishing.

VARIATION: COOL BLUE FLORAL

Red, yellow, and orange are warm colors; blue and green are cool colors. This variation uses exactly the same pattern as Art Deco Floral but employs a cooler palette. Turquoise and yellow replace red and orange as flower petal colors. Thin light green lines highlight the yellow central petals and lower their temperature. Rich aquamarine replaces light orange as the background color. The leaves, already a cool green, are identical to Art Deco Floral.

VARNISHING TIPS

At each stage, apply a coat of varnish to seal in the work already done. In this way, everything under the varnish is protected. If you change your mind or make a mistake, you can use a damp cloth or paper towel to remove paint or glaze back to the varnish. Always let paint dry thoroughly before varnishing. You can varnish only the section you have just painted or the whole piece, whichever makes sense.

BATIK TECHNIQUE

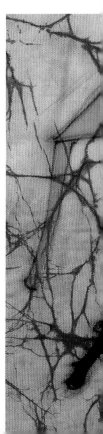

I N S P I R A T I O N *Many cultures produce batik fabrics. Our illustration shows an example of African folk art that uses the process. India also produces a variety of batik yard goods. The batik process involves applying dye to waxed fabric to form designs. Waxed fabric resists the dye. Unwaxed sections allow the dye to "take." The crackled effect is produced when the waxed fabric is crinkled, allowing the dye to penetrate.*

Decorative painters often use paint to imitate classic textures and finishes. The background of our oval box simulates the crinkled batik look. Traditionally, batik fabric was colored with plant dyes, producing warm, earthy tones and a range of blues. We chose a warm yellow, similar to the gold in the African work. Then we ratcheted up the palette with a bright turquoise and a deep blue. Ordinary clear plastic wrap replaces wax as the texturing agent.

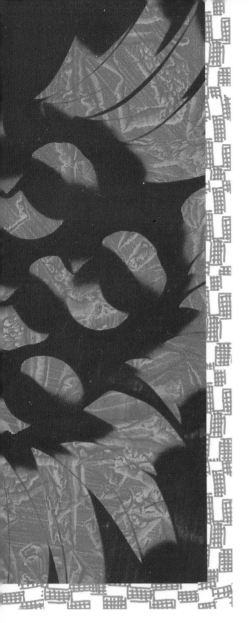

To create the basic batik texture, plastic wrap is used as a stamp.

Wooden or cardboard oval boxes are easy to find at craft stores. You might use a hat box or a square box with a lid. A lid lends itself to a decorative band. You might be tempted to use a cardboard box, but such a surface may not accept paint well or may not endure.

A wide band of the floral pattern surrounds the top half of the box. A band of batik texture remains untouched, and a checkerboard pattern surrounds the base.

This project uses art tools you may not be familiar with—from ordinary plastic wrap to the more exotic Colour Shaper. To create the basic batik texture, plastic wrap is used as a stamp. Different brands of wrap produce different effects, so experiment. One good feature of plastic wrap is that you don't need to wash it—just throw it away. Colour Shapers are also easy to clean but are as expensive as good brushes, so select carefully. Plastic wrap and Colour Shapers require some practice to use, but once you see the results, you will use them over and over.

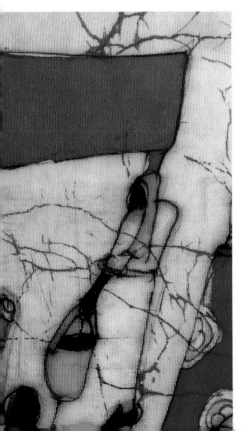

TOOLS AND MATERIALS

Wooden or cardboard oval or round box, or other object large enough to accommodate this combination of colors and patterns

brushes: a broad brush, approximately 1"(2.5 cm); #1; # 4 and #6 script liners, a #4 flat shader; and a 1" (2.5 cm) sponge brush (or brushes that achieve similar effects)

#6 chisel Colour Shaper

sealer-primer

water-based flow acrylic paints: yellow, deep blue, and turquoise

water-based varnish

extender or blending medium

clear plastic wrap

one or two sheets of Bristol board

newspaper or paper towel

sandpaper: medium grade (#150 or #400) and #600 superfine

This project uses a broad brush to apply glaze.

What could be simpler? The fun comes as you incise designs into the glaze with a Colour Shaper. In a sense, a Colour Shaper is the opposite of a brush in that it removes, rather than adds, color. Removing the glaze reveals the underlying color and texture. Short, square strokes form a checkerboard. Other strokes, such as zigzags and squiggles, remove most of the glaze but not all, creating a textured stroke. A #12 chisel Colour Shaper, a good size to start with, is used in this project.

1
The pattern shown requires the listed colors. You may wish to substitute other colors, but consider using a light, bright color as the base coat, a medium value for the batik coat, and a dark color for the final decoration. After choosing your color scheme, you may want to sketch the object and a possible design layout in preparation for a later step.

yellow

deep blue

turquoise

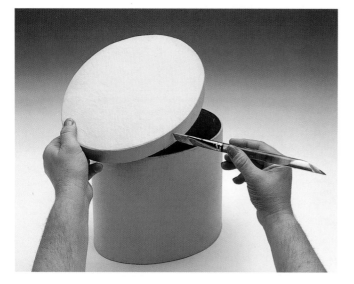

2
If the box is wood, sand and seal it, as shown in Surface Preparation. If you are working with cardboard, apply primer-sealer and three coats of varnish to assure that paint will not ripple the paper texture of the box. Dry thoroughly between coats. When the surface is smooth and firm, apply a yellow base coat with a 1" (2.5 cm) brush. Apply two coats of varnish. At the same time, apply a base coat and varnish to a sheet of Bristol board to use as a practice sheet.

3
To make the plastic wrap stamp, gather both ends of a 12" to 15" (31 cm to 38 cm) length of plastic wrap and pull it lengthwise so that it becomes a randomly pleated strip. Then, holding the strip in the thumb and fingers of one hand, wrap the strip loosely around those fingers with the other hand, forming a soft, crinkled wad of wrap that will be your stamping tool. Practice using the stamp so that you will be ready to work as soon as you apply the glaze.

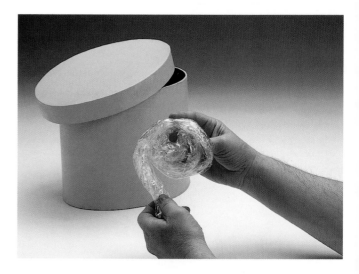

4 To keep the texture crisp, you will need to keep the stamp relatively clean. Have a section of newspaper or paper towel handy. When you notice paint building up on the stamp, blot it thoroughly on the newspaper or paper towel.

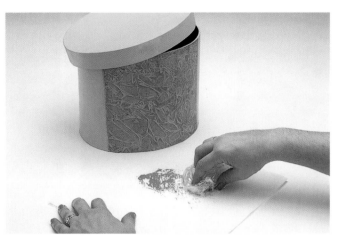

5 Mix a glaze by combining one part turquoise paint with one part extender. Practice glazing, stamping, and blotting on your Bristol board before working on your box. Mentally divide the box into workable areas. For example, the top of the lid, the band of the lid, one side, the other side, and the bottom. Do not cover too large an area because the glaze may dry and become unworkable. Using a 1" (2.5 cm) brush, apply the wet, but not runny, glaze quickly and evenly to a portion of the box.

6 Quickly form the stamp. Press it firmly into the wet glaze and remove it, leaving the batik texture. Change the angle of the stamp to vary the texture. Move to an adjacent area and continue until you have textured the glazed portion. Blot frequently and move on. Try not to leave a harsh line between sections. You can improve imperfect texture by quickly refreshing the glaze and restamping. When the texture is dry, apply two coats of varnish with a foam or soft bristle brush, making sure each coat dries thoroughly.

COLOUR SHAPER TIPS

Colour Shapers are used to remove glaze from a painted surface that has been protected with varnish. Enjoy experimenting with Shapers on various backgrounds and glazes. Press down firmly on the Shaper to make a clean sweep. Wipe the tip on a paper towel frequently to keep it clean. If you are not satisfied with your Colour Shaping, "erase" it by quickly reapplying glaze. If you still don't like your work, wipe off the glaze back to the varnished surface and start again.

7 Prepare a second glaze by mixing one part dark blue paint with one part extender. With the 1" (2.5 cm) brush, apply the glaze to your practice sheet. Practice using the #6 chisel Colour Shaper to form patterns: small circles or pairs of curved strokes, squiggles, and short petal shapes. The concave side of the Colour Shaper scrapes the glaze off the varnished surface to reveal the underlying texture.

8 Now it is time to decide how you will apply designs to your box. Sketch out your design. Our lid is covered with floral shapes made up of the small circles and petals practiced earlier. The squiggles will decorate the band on the lid.

9 The checkerboard pattern is the easiest to execute, so you might prefer to complete that before moving on to the more complex flower pattern. Leave a thin band of batik texture below the area on which you will add the floral shapes, then apply a band of dark blue glaze at the base of the box. Use the Colour Shaper to remove alternating rectangles of glaze. You could decorate the entire box using only areas of batik texture and bands of squiggles and checkerboard.

GLAZE TIPS

We recommend a glaze of one part paint to one part extender. However, some paints are more transparent than others. You may need to adjust proportions. Adding more extender adds transparency. Always test the consistency of your glaze. If it is too thin, it will run back into the shape you have created. If it is too thick, it may dry too quickly to work with.

10 Apply the blue glaze to the top of the lid and implement the floral pattern you practiced in step 7. To assure an even distribution of flowers, you might use a small circle as a marker for the center of each flower and then develop the flower around that center. After you have completed the lid, apply a band of floral pattern around the top third of the box itself.

11 Apply blue glaze to the band of the lid. Use the Colour Shaper to create the squiggle pattern. When you are pleased with your design, varnish and wet sand the box, as described in Surface Preparation and Finishing.

VARIATION: DEEP BATIK

This pattern uses exactly the same techniques with different colors. Apply a dark turquoise batik texture over the yellow base coat. Then prepare an orange glaze and paint large squares over the texture. After the orange glaze is thoroughly dry, paint wide bands of dark blue glaze and, with the Colour Shaper, incise a complex pattern into the bands.

VICTORIAN BEADS

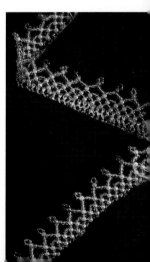

INSPIRATION *In many Victorian boudoirs, candle or kerosene flames shed their glow through beaded lampshades. Generally smaller than parlor lamps with stained glass shades, they were no less radiant, even after electrification. The beading tended toward simple geometric shapes, relying on the color and luminosity of the beads to create their effect. In the 1920s, candlesticks with beaded shades added glitter to Parisian night clubs.*

Our updated version recreates the Victorian lamp effect, using bright "beads" of paint in layered geometric patterns to decorate the shade. One element of the pattern links the candlestick base to the shade. Another lamp base, such as a ginger jar, would do as well. The shade is made of coated paper. If the shade on your lamp is fabric, you will need to replace it with a coated paper shade, as this technique is designed for a smooth surface.

The focus for this project is color—glowing, glorious color.

The focus for this project is color—glowing, glorious color. Light shining through the shade and onto the base enhances the effect. Even in daylight, the juxtaposition of yellow-green, red-violet, red-orange, yellow-orange, turquoise, violet, light violet, and deep blue dazzle the eyes. Glazes made of paint thinned with extender contribute almost transparent radiance.

Most of these colors are applied in straight strokes to build geometric forms. Short and long stripes tend to be broad and straight, so you can be bold. No fine lines or tricky curves here. Even so, you will want to sketch your design before painting.

Bright colors are set against bands of an airy texture created with bubble wrap. Suspend your disbelief until you see how simple this stamping process is. Once you try it, you will want to use bubble-wrap textures on other projects.

The base is balanced and basic. Clear colors coordinate with the shade, while an easy checkerboard pattern provides interest. If you want to light up a dim corner or brighten your spirits, this lamp has the wattage.

TOOLS AND MATERIALS

lamp and coated paper lamp shade

brushes: a broad brush, approximately 1" (2.5 cm); #1, #4, and #6 script liners, a #4 flat shader; and a 1" (2.5 cm) sponge brush (or brushes that achieve similar effects)

sealer-primer

water-based flow acrylic paints: yellow-green, red-violet, red-orange, yellow-orange, turquoise, violet, light violet, and deep blue

water-based varnish

extender or blending medium

bubble wrap with 1" (2.5 cm) air pockets

chalk or quilter's pencil (optional)

sandpaper: medium grade (#150 or #400) and #600 superfine

Brushstrokes for this project couldn't be simpler.

If you can paint a straight line and even if you can't, you are all set. Brushes of varying types and width do all the work to create lines, squares, rectangles, triangles, and bands of color. Because you will be able to execute the brushstrokes easily, you can relax and enjoy playing with the luminous, dancing colors.

1

Because this pattern simulates brightly hued beads, it calls for many luminous colors. You could substitute others but, because so many are juxtaposed, be sure to work out the combinations in advance. Prepare a sketch of the lamp and of the shade. It may be helpful to sketch the shade in perspective and also make a template, either to scale or full size. Later you will be able to fold the template to assure an even distribution of the pattern.

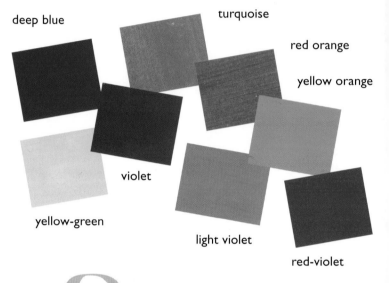

deep blue   turquoise   red orange   yellow orange   violet   yellow-green   light violet   red-violet

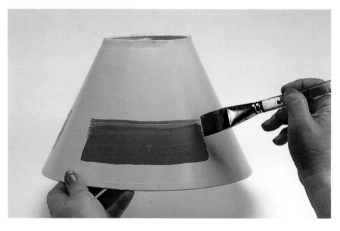

2

Use the 1" (2.5 cm) brush to apply a yellow-green base coat to the base and to the shade. Paint the bottom of the lamp pedestal deep blue. After the paint has dried, apply two coats of varnish, making sure the first is dry before applying the second. Cut a piece of bubble wrap approximately 12" (31 cm) x 4" (10 cm). This will be used to stamp circular shapes into the glaze. Then prepare a glaze of one part red-violet paint and one part extender. Apply a broad band of glaze halfway around the base of the shade; it is better to texture one section at a time.

3

Press the bubble wrap firmly into the wet glaze. You will see a pattern emerging as each bubble crinkles into the glaze. Peel the bubble wrap off smoothly, blot it on a paper towel or newspaper to remove excess paint and move it to the next glazed area of the stripe. Glaze and texture the remaining half of the band. When you have completed that band, repeat the process of glazing and bubble wrapping a band near the top of the shade. After both bands are dry, apply two coats of varnish to the textured stripes.

4 Prepare a second glaze by mixing one part turquoise paint with one part extender. Using a 1" (2.5 cm) flat brush, paint a strip around the top of the upper band, overlapping the yellow-green base coat and the rose-violet bubble-wrap texture. Repeat this glazed strip at the bottom of the lower band. You may want to practice this and the following steps on palette paper or varnished Bristol board before working on your shade. Notice how the glaze transforms both colors. Apply two coats of varnish to these newly glazed areas when they are dry.

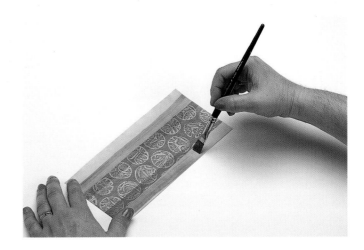

5 Prepare a third glaze by mixing one part red-orange paint with one part extender. Using the #12 flat shader, paint stripes of red-orange glaze that bisect the remaining bubble wrap textured bands. Again note the effect of the glaze on the colors beneath. Apply two coats of varnish over the stripes.

6 Prepare a fourth glaze by mixing one part yellow-orange paint with one part extender. Using the #12 flat shader, paint triangles, broad base down, around the bottom of the shade, extending from $\frac{1}{2}$" (1.3 cm) below the band of turquoise glaze to the top of the red-violet band. You may wish to use your template to measure off even spaces and mark them very lightly on the shade with chalk, a quilter's pencil, or dots of the yellow-orange glaze. Apply two coats of varnish to seal the triangles.

SURFACE PREPARATION TIPS

If the base is unfinished wood, sand and seal it, as described in Surface Preparation and Finishing. More likely, you will be working with a used lamp with a metal or finished wood surface. If the base is metal, prepare it with metal primer. If the base is finished wood, sand it to remove any loose finish and to degloss the surface so that it will receive the base coat well. If the lamp shade is worn, it would be wise to purchase a new coated paper shade.

7 Using violet paint and a #6 flat shader, bead the top edges of the yellow-orange triangles with short rectangular strokes, forming a zigzag pattern. You could do this freehand or mark a guide with the quilter's pencil.

8 Use light violet paint (violet mixed with white) and a #12 flat shader to paint even stripes in the bands of yellow-green base coat that are still exposed halfway down the shade. After all the paint is dry, apply two coats of varnish to the entire shade. Embellish it still further by adding deep blue stripes to the top and bottom bands. It is not necessary to wet sand the shade; doing so may damage it.

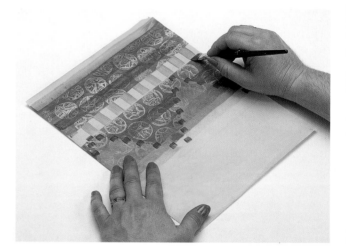

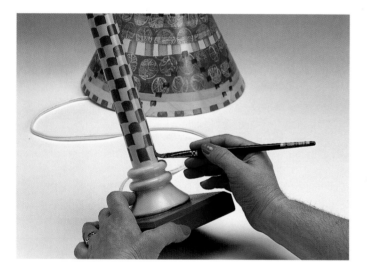

9 You have already base coated and varnished the lamp base in step 2. Now, using the violet paint, create a checkerboard effect on the lamp base by alternating short strokes with the #12 flat shader.

BUBBLE-WRAP TIPS

Bubble wrap is an air-filled cellophane product used to protect items during handling or shipping. The most common size is made up of air-filled pockets only 1/2" (1.3 cm) in diameter. The size used in this pattern contains bubbles that are 1" (2.5 cm) wide bubbles. When cutting bubble wrap, you may need to weave between the bubbles to avoid puncturing them. Check to see that all bubbles are filled with air. Airless pockets do not make interesting prints.

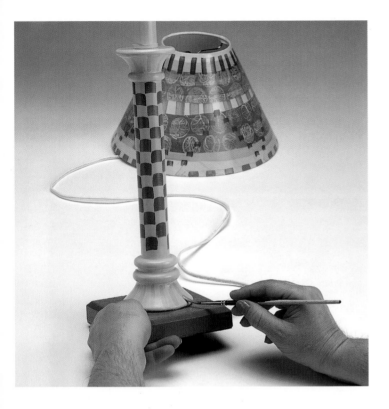

10 Use a #6 script liner to paint yellow-orange stripes on the flared lower and upper lips of the base. These simple strokes, along with the checkerboard, provide color links to the shade. Varnish and wet sand the base, as described in Surface Preparation and Finishing.

VARIATION: GLOWING BEADS

This pattern glows with the same colors shown on the lampshade. The same procedures are used to create bands of orange, red-violet, and turquoise glaze that overlap and partially cover the same bright yellow base coat. In this variation, the bubble-wrap stripe has disappeared. Instead, wide bands of light violet glaze cover the brightly colored bands. In contrast to painting "beads," a Colour Shaper was used to remove small squares of the light violet glaze to reveal the colors beneath. See Batik Technique for tips on using the Colour Shaper.

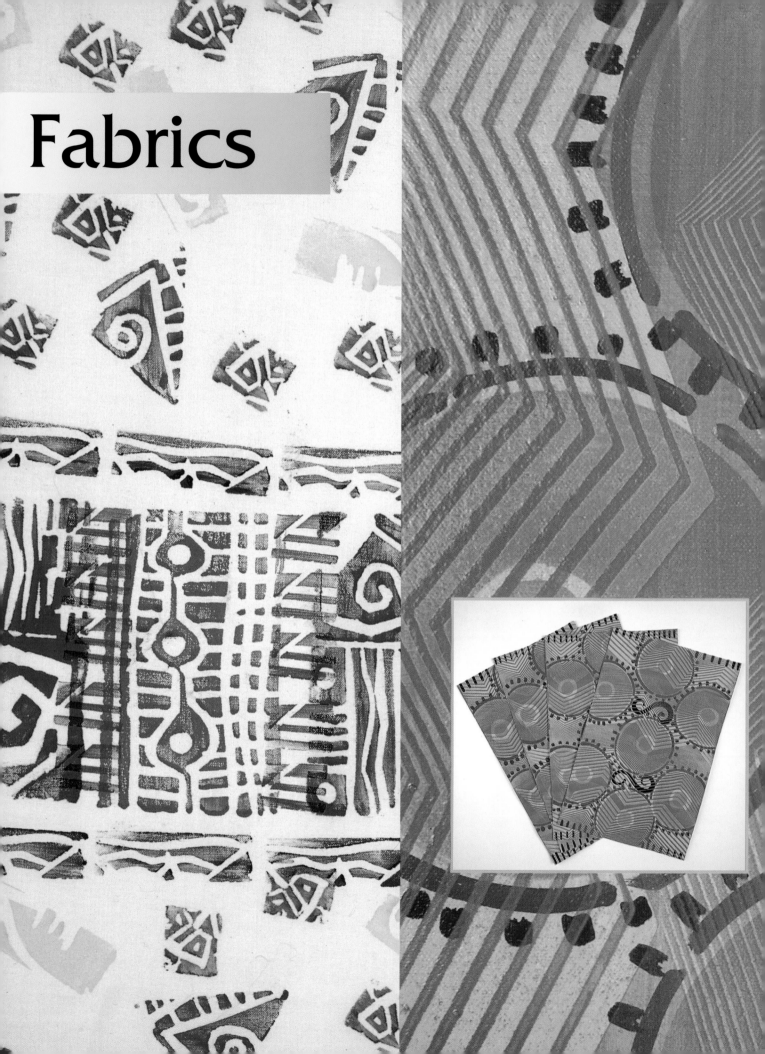

Fabrics

PERUVIAN PATTERNS

INSPIRATION *A Peruvian textile exhibit inspired the rich color schemes and decorative motifs used for this fabric pattern. The ancient Peruvians wove yarns dyed bright organic colors into intricate patterns for garments and religious items. Because of the limitations of the weaving process, linear designs prevailed. Despite this, the imaginative motifs, sophisticated variety, juxtaposition of patterns, and bright colors ensured a lively effect.*

Our printed fabric borrows design motifs from traditional Peruvian weaving. Small geometric forms dance on the fabric like angular polka dots. These small stamped forms sometimes resemble tiny animals—perhaps a snake or a snail. Larger abstract motifs combine to form a border.

Pure, bright primary and secondary colors combine to create a cheerful pattern.

Peruvian weavers were limited to colors they could derive from plants and other natural sources. The modern artist enjoys broader color choices. In this case, pure, bright primary and secondary colors combine to create a cheerful pattern. Begin by sketching motif ideas. When you have several that please you, try putting them together in various combinations and again sketch out pattern ideas that these combinations may suggest. Next, incise both small and large motifs onto rubber printing blocks with a linoleum cutter. For the pattern shown, you will need four small blocks: a triangle 2" high (5 cm), a small square 1" x 1" (2.5 cm x 2.5 cm), and two rectangles about $^3/_4$"x 2" (2 cm x 5.5 cm). The two larger blocks are 4" x 4" (10 cm x 10 cm) and 4" x $2^1/_2$" (10 cm x 6.5 cm).

You can mount the stamps on wooden blocks to make them easier to handle. After deciding on your colors, apply paint onto the surface of the block and press it firmly onto the fabric. With this simple and satisfying process, you can create fabric that has exactly the color and pattern effects you wish to achieve.

TOOLS AND MATERIALS

cotton muslin or other natural-fiber fabric that will accept paint, 1 yard (90 cm) or more

brushes: a broad brush, approximately 1" (2.5 cm)

rubber printing blocks for making stamps. A 9" x 12" (23 cm x 30 cm) or other large block can be cut into smaller sizes

wooden blocks to make handles for small stamps. These can be cut from a $^1/_2$" to $^5/_8$" thick (1.3 to 1.5 cm thick) board

hot glue gun or other adhesive

linoleum-cutting tool

craft knife

water-based flow acrylic paints: red, orange, yellow, green, and blue

tape or quilter's pencil

iron

Stamping requires no fancy brushwork.

You simply use a 1" (2.5 cm) brush to apply paint to the stamp and press the stamp firmly onto the fabric. For this pattern, you will use three small stamps—a triangle, a square, and a rectangle—for the red, green, and yellow Peruvian "polka dots"; a small rectangular block for the blue, wave-like pattern; and two larger rectangular blocks for the orange and green geometric patterns.

1 Choose a palette of bright primary and secondary colors and paint swatches of the colors near each other on palette paper. Primary colors are red, yellow, and blue. Secondary colors are created by mixing two primaries: Red and yellow form orange; blue and yellow form green. You will not need to mix paints to create green and orange; both are readily available right out of the bottle.

orange   yellow   green   red   blue

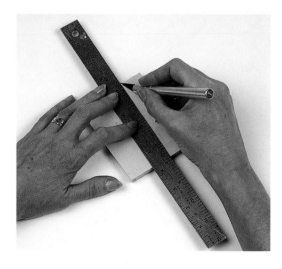

2 After you have decided on your design elements, cut the large rubber block into appropriate sizes with a craft knife.

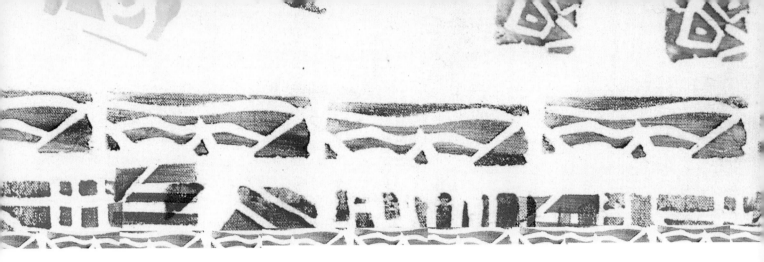

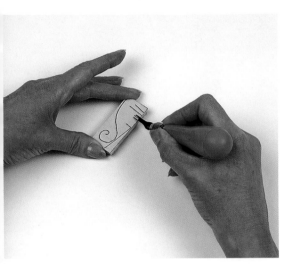

Draw a design onto each block with a pencil. Then use the linoleum-cutting tool to incise the design. Be conservative in removing the rubber, remembering that what you leave forms the printing surface. You can always remove more rubber to increase negative space. Use a glue gun or other adhesive to attach a block of wood to the backs of the small stamps. This makes them easier to hold and to press.

Use a 1" (2.5 cm) brush to apply a thin layer of paint to one stamp. Test the stamp on paper or extra fabric. If the design is clear, you are ready to repaint the block and stamp the fabric. If the design is not as crisp as you'd like, cut away a little more rubber. As you print, be careful not to get paint in the carved-out lines. If you do, get rid of it with a clean brush.

Start by using the three small stamps in red, yellow, and green to create a random pattern. Select the triangular stamp and apply red paint. Press the stamp firmly and evenly onto the fabric to transfer the paint. Remove the stamp by lifting it straight up. If you want to print a border, mark its location with tape or a quilter's pencil to save the space for printing later on.

5 Continue random stamping with the triangle in the area to be patterned. Repeat with the square block and blue paint, and with the rectangular stamp and yellow paint to form an overall design. Be sure to wait until one color is dry before applying the next. It is perfectly acceptable to overlap the stamps occasionally.

6 The border shown is $5^1/_2$" (14 cm) wide. In step 4, we explained how to indicate its edges as you are stamping the rest of the fabric. Use the small rectangular wave-like stamp and blue paint to edge the border.

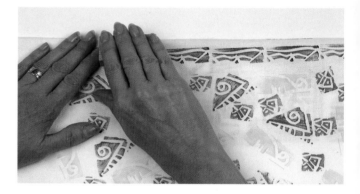

7 The pattern calls for printing the two larger stamps alternately: the large rectangle and orange paint, then the large square and green paint. It is best to print one color at a time. Start by printing the green block. Place the clean rectangular block to the right of the green block just printed, as a marker. Continue in this way, printing green blocks in alternate spaces. Then fill in the empty spaces by printing the orange rectangles. When the paint is thoroughly dry, iron the fabric to set the paint. With the iron set at "cotton," place a clean cloth over the fabric, print side up, and iron.

VARIATION: PERUVIAN PEACH

Similar stamps decorate this variation printed on peach-colored polished cotton. The polka dots in this case are light terra cotta, periwinkle blue, and black. Black stamps edge the broad border, which is printed with larger stamps, alternating brown, black, and periwinkle. The border is transformed by over-painting with a lavender wash. Mix the wash by combining one part paint with four parts water.

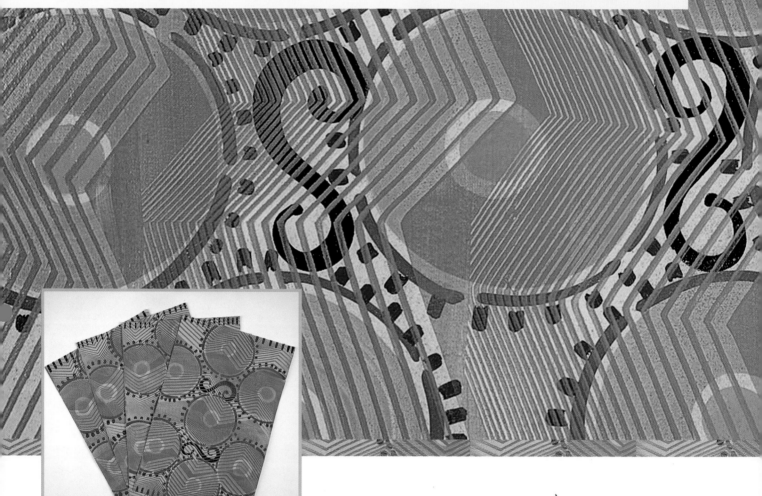

BASICALLY BOKHARA

INSPIRATION *Weavers from Bokhara, a village in what is now the Uzbekistan region of Russia, have produced magnificent carpets for centuries. Their art peaked in the nineteenth century, and since then, traditional Bokhara patterns have been widely copied in other weaving centers, such as Pakistan.*

The placemat pattern shown here is based on the stunning patterns of Ikat, a textile process perfected in Bokhara. Orange, red, green, and gold combine in a bold pattern full of sinuous curves.

The same pattern and technique could be used for larger pieces.

Our stylized Bokhara design underlies a combed-glaze surface to create contemporary canvas placemats that could as easily adorn a picnic table as a gracious dining table. In reality, these are mini floor cloths, and the same pattern and technique could be used for larger pieces, such as area rugs for hallways and bathrooms, wall-hangings, or table runners.

Begin by sketching the design. Large concentric circles form the dominant medallion shapes. The circles are painted in various colors, using different forms—that is, a solid, a wide band, a narrow broken band, and dotted lines. Sinuous *S* shapes frame the central circle, and short lines form a fringe at the edges. Finally, several coats of varnish assure that this art for the table will resist spills and stains.

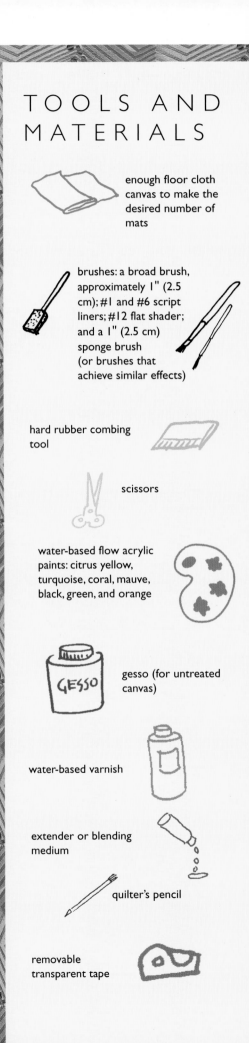

TOOLS AND MATERIALS

enough floor cloth canvas to make the desired number of mats

brushes: a broad brush, approximately 1" (2.5 cm); #1 and #6 script liners; #12 flat shader; and a 1" (2.5 cm) sponge brush (or brushes that achieve similar effects)

hard rubber combing tool

scissors

water-based flow acrylic paints: citrus yellow, turquoise, coral, mauve, black, green, and orange

gesso (for untreated canvas)

water-based varnish

extender or blending medium

quilter's pencil

removable transparent tape

This project calls for simple brush strokes.
Use the #6 script liner to form the green kidney beans. The same brush and a little brush control create the large *S* shapes. The mauve arc also calls for the #6 script liner. The arc is just a curved line with slight pressure applied at the start and finish.

1 Choose the colors you want to use for your placemats and paint combinations of them on a piece of palette paper. Here, the color scheme includes an underpainting of citrus yellow, with circle elements in coral, turquoise, mauve, and green. The *S* shapes and fringe are black. A combed orange glaze creates a woven effect.

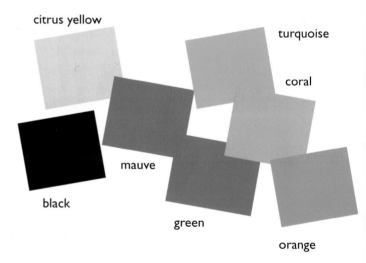

citrus yellow

turquoise

coral

mauve

black

green

orange

2 Treated floor cloth canvas requires no priming. If you are using untreated canvas, use a broad brush to apply one coat of gesso to the back and two coats to the top of the canvas, making sure the first coat is dry before applying the second. Cut the canvas to the desired size and shape. The mats shown are 17" x 11" (43 cm x 28 cm). Use a 1" (2.5 cm) brush and citrus green paint to base-coat the double-primed surface of the mats.

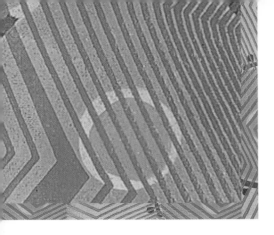

COMBING TIPS

A professional (moderately expensive), hard rubber combing tool achieves the effect shown. Make your own tools from the bottom of a polyfoam grocer's tray or a rubber spatula cut with pinking shears. Apply the glaze evenly. Too much glaze will run and your texture will not be crisp; too little will dry before you can work the comb through it. Press the comb firmly as you rake across the glaze to achieve a clean pattern. Wipe the comb frequently to keep it clean.

3 Cut a cardboard circle about 4" (10 cm) in diameter to use as a template. Place the template on the center of the mat and use the quilter's pencil to trace around it. Then surround the central circle with six other circles, each slightly overlapping the edge of the mat. Use the 1" (2.5 cm) brush to paint turquoise donuts, using the circle you have drawn as a guide.

4 Use a #12 flat shader to paint coral circles within the donut, leaving a circle of citrus yellow showing. Then use the #6 script liner to form a series of mauve arcs around the donut. To create a more interesting arc, press the brush down slightly as you begin and end the stroke.

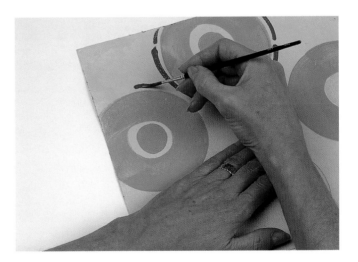

5 Use the #6 script liner and green paint to outline each circle with green kidney beans. Using the same brush, paint a black fringe of short dashes at the right and left edges of the mat. Still using the #6 script liner and black paint, paint a large *S* on either side of the central circle. If you want monogrammed mats, you might insert your own initials. After the painting is completely dry, apply two coats of varnish.

6 Mix a glaze that is one part orange paint and one part extender. Apply the glaze evenly to about a third of the mat, making sure there are no puddles or uncovered areas. Then use the combing tool in a zigzag motion to form the texture. You could use a waving motion for a different effect. For tips on combing, see page 55. Apply at least five more coats of varnish to the painting, making sure each coat dries before applying the next, to create a glorious and highly resistant surface. Be sure to varnish the edges of the mats and to apply one coat of varnish to the back, to protect your work.

VARIATION: BOKHARA BORDER

This variation shows how a simple extra step can add a new dimension to your pattern. Use removable transparent tape to mask the mat, forming an open rectangle at each of its edges. Press the tape down firmly with your fingernail to ensure a tight seal. Mix a fuchsia glaze and apply it to each rectangle with a 1" (2.5 cm) brush. When the glaze is dry, remove the tape. Notice the color transformation. Some colors seem to recede, and the turquoise has transformed to purple.

MIRO MAGIC

INSPIRATION *The Spanish surrealist, Joan Miro, painted with playful spontaneity. The result was a body of work that conveyed a naive, almost childlike, charm. He often used linear forms or simple, flat-colored shapes outlined with white or black that danced across a background that shades from one color into another. Despite the surface simplicity, Miro's work invites symbolic or poetic interpretations.*

Our whimsical interpretation of Miro's style combines hazy washes blending into each other, random dancing shapes, and impromptu calligraphic doodles.

Sketch your designs for stamps on paper first.

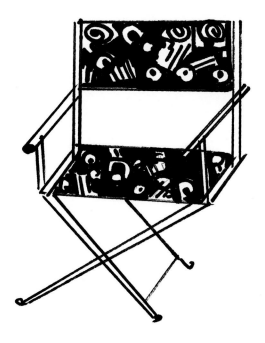

Director's chairs provide convenient, spontaneous seating. Why not decorate the canvas covers of a director's chair to add unique character to practicality? You can easily obtain new chairs and covers from department stores and retail catalogs. If you already own a director's chair, you can purchase or make a new off-white cover, or you can use the cover you have and adapt your design to its color.

Our cover is made of untreated canvas in an off-white color. Stamps create the basic design elements. Sketch your designs for stamps on paper first. Although the design is informal and could be done freehand, you might also want to sketch possible layouts for the stamps and other design elements.

You can cut a simple circular stamp out of an ordinary household sponge. Other designs are carved into rubber printing blocks. After applying a random stamped pattern to the seat and back of the chair, use a marking pen to draw freehand line designs between and on top of your stamped pattern. Background colors are then added as washes.

TOOLS AND MATERIALS

 director's chair with heavyweight untreated cotton canvas seat and back

brushes: a broad brush, approximately 1" (2.5 cm); #1 script liners; a #12 flat shader; and a 2" (5 cm) sponge brush (or brushes that achieve similar effects)

 ordinary cellulose kitchen sponge

scissors

medium-point permanent black marking pen

rubber printing block, cut to the desired sizes

craft knife

linoleum-cutting tool

water-based flow acrylic paints: light terra cotta, Asia blue, red iron oxide, turquoise, blue, and citrus green

iron

water-repellent fabric protector (optional)

Stamps really do all the work.

The only painting involves painting blocks for stamping and applying washes with a broad brush. Cut the circular stamp from a sponge and print the Asia-blue donuts. Other designs are from rubber stamps, using light terra cotta, red iron oxide, and turquoise paints. Black free-form doodles drawn with a marking pen add the Miro flair.

1 Determine the colors you want to use and create a paper palette with small examples of the colors. A black permanent marking pen is used to add free, impulsive, doodle-like designs in the style of Miro. Finally, the background colors are painted on in a sequence of blue and citrus green washes.

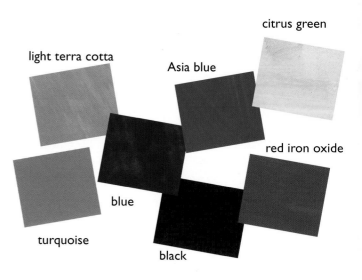

citrus green

light terra cotta

Asia blue

red iron oxide

blue

turquoise

black

2 Cut a 2" (5 cm) circle from an ordinary household cellulose sponge. Remove a 1" (2.5 cm) center from one surface, forming a small donut-shaped printing surface. Use the 1" (2.5 cm) brush to paint one side of the sponge Asia blue. Do not overload the sponge. Press the sponge down on the fabric firmly and lift it up carefully. Print circles in a random pattern, leaving plenty of room for other motifs. Reload the sponge with paint before each stamping.

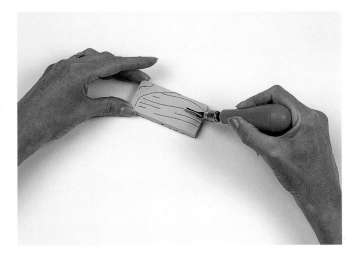

Cut three blocks from the rubber printing block: 1" x 2" (2.5 cm x 5 cm) for the light terra cotta toothbrush design, 1" x 2 ¼" (2.5 cm x 5.6 cm) for the red iron oxide eye design, and 4" x 2 ½" (10 cm x 6.25 cm) for the turquoise linear design. Draw a design onto each block with a pencil. Then use the linoleum-cutting tool to incise the design. Be conservative in removing the rubber, remembering that what you leave forms the printing surface. You can always remove more rubber to increase negative space. If you have not used printing blocks before, please read the tip box on page 60.

Use the 1" (2.5 cm) brush to load turquoise paint onto the largest block. Apply the block to the fabric and press down firmly. Remove the block carefully. Reload and print in a random pattern, leaving plenty of space in between.

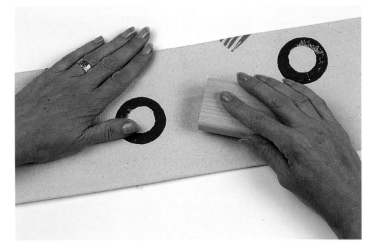

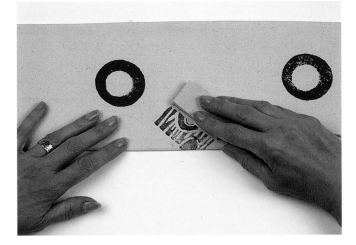

Paint the 1" x 2¼" (3.1 cm x 5.6 cm) block with red iron oxide paint. Print as before, allowing room to turn the block to stamp another facing design. Notice that by using the same rectangular block twice, you can form a more complex square motif. Again, leave plenty of space between squares.

6 You have two more design elements to add—the smallest of the three stamps and the doodles made with the marker—so allot the remaining space accordingly. Load the smallest, toothbrush-patterned, stamp with light terra cotta paint. Print randomly as before, leaving space for the marker doodles.

7 After all the stamping designs are thoroughly dry, use the black permanent marker to add linear Miro-like doodles in the remaining space. You may want to try this on scrap fabric first, to loosen up. To prevent the ink from bleeding, be careful not to press down too firmly or leave the marker in one place too long.

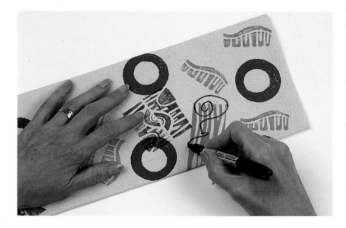

8 Mix the two washes, blue and citrus green, in separate containers. (You will also need a container of water to rinse your brush.) A wash is very thin paint prepared by mixing four parts water with one part paint. Dip the 1" (2.5 cm) brush in the blue wash and paint a broad stripe of more than 2" (5 cm). Rinse the brush in water.

TIPS ON DESIGNING STAMPS

Consider the scale of your piece when deciding on the sizes of your stamps. Very large stamps (larger than 4", or 10 cm) or very small stamps (smaller than 1", or 2.5 cm) are often hard to handle. Because simple designs usually print more clearly than complex designs, consider designing stamps that you can use alone or in combination to form a more complex pattern. The red iron oxide stamp shown in Step 5 is an example of a double-duty stamp.

Load the brush with the citrus green wash. Paint a stripe overlapping some of the right edge of the wet blue wash to form a darker green. Rinse the brush and continue painting a continuation of the citrus stripe, another 3" (7.5 cm) or so. Rinse the brush again and paint blue wash over some of the yellow wash to form green. Rinse and add a blue stripe. Continue alternating blue and citrus washes across the chair cover, creating green blending in between.

When the fabric is completely dry, use an iron at the "cotton" setting to set the colors. Place the cover, painted-side up on the ironing board, cover it with a clean cloth, and iron. If your chair may occasionally be exposed to the weather or if you anticipate spills, you might wish to treat the fabric with water-repellent fabric protector.

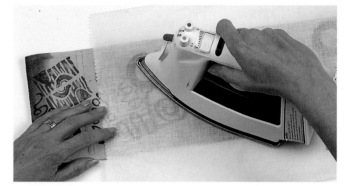

VARIATION: MAGENTA MIRO

This variation uses the same stamping, marker doodling, and wash process as the project above. Carved stamps print magenta, red, olive green, black, citrus green, and goldenrod designs. The donut sponge stamp prints a black design, and the black marker creates the doodles. A magenta wash, applied in large squares and rectangles alters the underlying printed pattern.

MATISSE MANNER

INSPIRATION *The clear bright color, simple elegant shapes, and bold patterns of the work of Henri Matisse was the inspiration for this floor cloth design. Toward the end of his life, when he was too ill to stand at the easel, he "painted" with colored paper cut into inventive abstract shapes and, in this way, he created marvelous collages.*

In this Matisse-inspired rendering and in other works of his period, natural objects, such as leaves and fish, were reduced to their simplest forms and combined with patterns of pure color and interesting shapes, such as spirals and irregular curved lines. This project uses turquoise leafy shapes against a bright yellow-orange ground as an underpainting for a floor cloth.

Prepare a working sketch before beginning to paint.

Traditionally, painted floor cloths have simulated rug patterns and substituted for more expensive carpets. Today, decorators and homeowners use painted floor cloths as durable and attractive hallway accents or even as the foundation for decorating an entire room.

The basic material for the floor cloth is heavy cotton canvas, double primed on one side, single primed on the other. If you cannot purchase prepared floor cloth canvas, you can prime canvas with gesso. A painted floor cloth represents an investment in material and time because of its scale, so prepare a working sketch before beginning to paint.

Some of the basic underpainting shapes, Matisse-like leaves, crescents, and squares, are painted in flat colors; others are textured with bubble wrap or highlighted with short lines. Removable tape delineates panels glazed in deep blue-violet and then incised with shapes and squiggles by the Colour Shaper, revealing some of the under-painting. Deep blue-violet highlights complete the piece. This technique and pattern could also be used for placemats and wallhangings.

TOOLS AND MATERIALS

heavyweight cotton floor cloth canvas; 3' x 2' (.9 meters x .6 meters) for a small floor cloth or enough to suit your project

brushes: a broad brush, approximately 1" (2.5 cm); #1 script liners; a #12 flat shader; and a 2" (5 cm) sponge brush (or brushes that achieve similar effects)

cardboard or other paper for cutting templates

6 and #12 flat chisel Colour Shapers

gesso (if your canvas is not primed)

water-based flow acrylic paints: yellow-orange, turquoise, black, light purple, red iron oxide, deep turquoise, and deep blue-violet

extender or blending medium

water-based varnish

removable transparent tape

bubble wrap with 1" (2.5 cm) bubbles

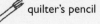
quilter's pencil

Matisse used simple forms and we use simple strokes.

Besides filling in leaf shapes, the only brush strokes are small, light purple squares produced with the #12 flat shader and black lines made with the #1 script liner. Colour Shapers in #6 and #10 sizes produce squiggles, lines, ribbons, and pine tree shapes.

1 Select your palette. The design shown employs bright colors. You might choose another combination, but it is wise to use a light, bright color for the base coat.

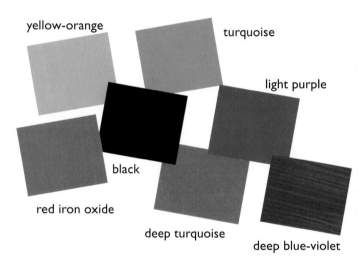

yellow-orange

turquoise

light purple

black

red iron oxide

deep turquoise

deep blue-violet

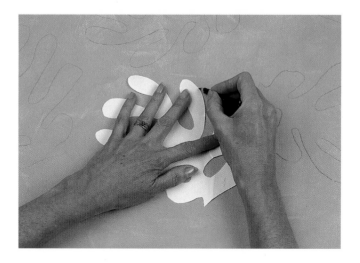

2 Cut the primed canvas to the desired size, in this case, approximately 2' x 3' (.6 meters x .9 meters). If the canvas is not primed, see the tip box. Use a 2" (5 cm) sponge brush and yellow-orange paint to base-coat the double-primed side of the canvas. Cut cardboard or paper into large Matisse-inspired leaf shapes. Outline the leaves on the floor cloth at various angles and directions, leaving space for more leaves in between.

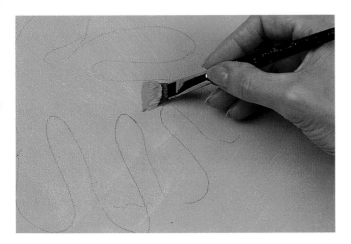

Use the 1" (2.5 cm) brush to paint the leaves turquoise. Wait for the paint to dry and then varnish the entire floor cloth. The varnish seals in the leaves and provides a base for glazing. The next step involves glazing and applying a bubble-wrap texture. If you have not done this before, you might want to read the tip box on bubble wrapping, in the Victorian Beads project.

Using the quilter's pencil, outline additional leaves, allowing some of the new leaves to overlap the turquoise leaves. Mix a glaze that is one part red iron oxide paint and one part extender. Then cut a piece of bubble wrap slightly larger than the leaf. Work on one leaf at a time. Use the 1" (2.5 cm) brush to apply a thin coat of glaze to the leaf shape. Press the bubble wrap into the glaze so that you can see wrinkles forming under each bubble. Peel off the bubble wrap and blot it to remove excess paint. Proceed to the remaining leaves.

Make a crescent-shaped template and outline crescents among the leaves. Mix a glaze that is one part teal paint and one part extender. Apply the glaze and use the bubble wrap to create a texture on the crescents, as you did with the leaves.

6 Use the #12 flat shader and light purple to paint small squares randomly on the remaining yellow-orange background. When the squares are dry, highlight each square with short black lines made with the #1 script liner. After all the paint has dried thoroughly, apply two coats of varnish to the entire floor cloth.

7 Use removable transparent tape to divide the floor cloth into an outside border and four central panels. Before applying tape, you might want to measure these borders and panels and mark them with a quilter's pencil. Run the edge of your fingernail along the edge of the tape to make sure no gaps or air pockets remain.

8 Mix a glaze that is one part blue-violet paint and one part extender. Work around the outer border first. With the 1" (2.5 cm) brush, apply the glaze thinly to one border section. Working quickly, use the #12 Colour Shaper to remove broad stripes of glaze, leaving glazed sections between the stripes to work the next design. Then use the #6 Colour Shaper in a tight back-and-forth zigzag motion to create pine tree shapes. Complete each border in the same manner.

TIPS ON PREPARING UNTREATED CANVAS

Priming seals and stiffens the fabric. If you can, purchase primed floor cloth canvas; otherwise, you can prime it yourself. If you are working with untreated canvas, apply gesso with a broad bristle or sponge brush. Apply two coats to the front or top of your floor cloth. Apply one coat to the back of your floor cloth.

Move to one of the center panels. Use the #6 Colour Shaper to create a random pattern of lines, squiggles, and ribbons. If you have not used the Colour Shaper before, read the tip box on page 35 and practice before working on the floor cloth. Continue with the remaining panels. When you are through, remove the tape carefully.

Use the #12 flat shader and deep blue-violet paint to highlight several areas in the panels and border. Apply five or more additional coats of varnish, depending on the use planned for your floor cloth. For example, one intended to cover the area in front of the kitchen sink might require many coats of varnish. Allow all coats to dry thoroughly before using your floor cloth.

VARIATION: GREEN MATISSE

The painted and bubble-wrap textured background in this variation is identical to the pattern shown above, but the palette is different. The base coat is pink; the leaves are lavender and orange. Fuchsia rectangles and black lines made with the permanent marker add detail. A green glaze covers the underpainting, except for the zigzags and ribbons incised with the Colour Shaper.

Furniture

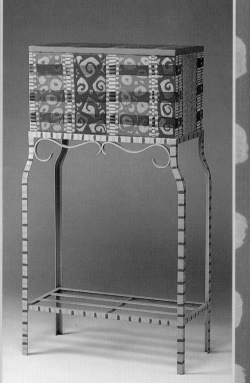

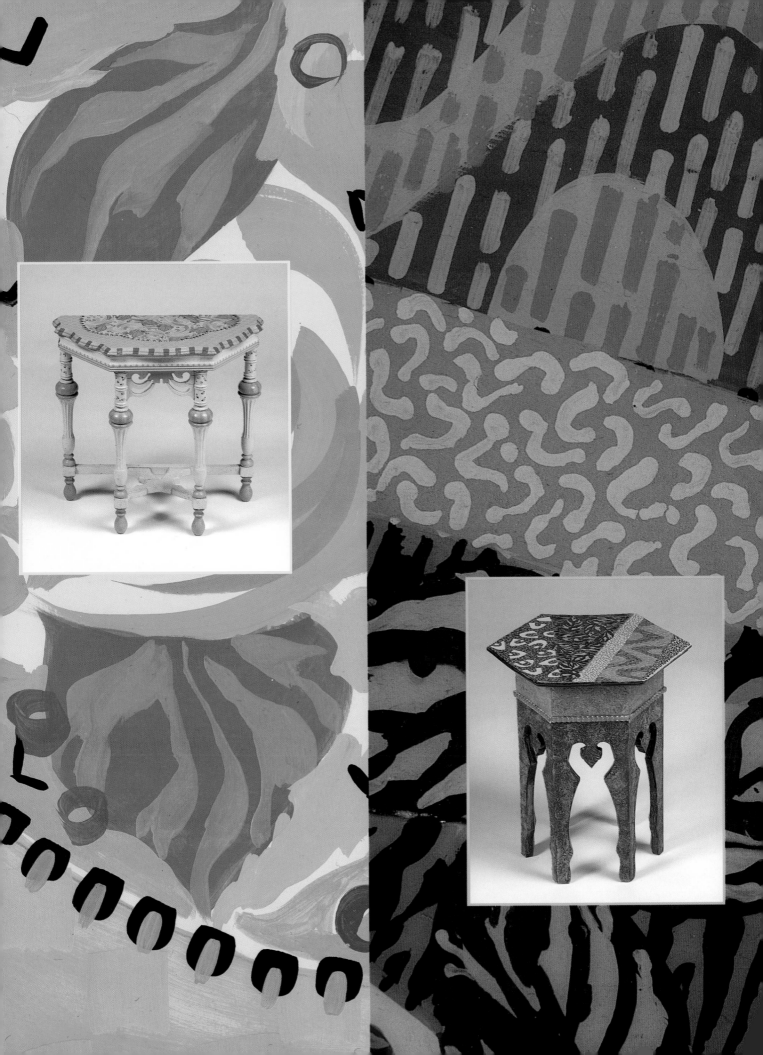

PHILODENDRON FANTASIA

INSPIRATION *The philodendron is a favorite houseplant because it grows in a variety of lighting conditions and thrives on neglect. More important, philodendrons display an abundance of glossy, verdant, heart-shaped leaves. You may have seen them as well-clipped specimens in tidy pots or as luxuriant trailers in hanging baskets. In their native environment, they have a vigorous, vine-like habit.*

Charles Eames's furniture designs helped define the bold, sleek '50s style. With the assistance of paints and brushes, we have persuaded philodendron vines to trail over the back of the classic Eames-style chair. The interpretation of the vines and the surrounding bands of pattern is definitely Deco.

The smooth surface of this armchair lends itself to decorative painting.

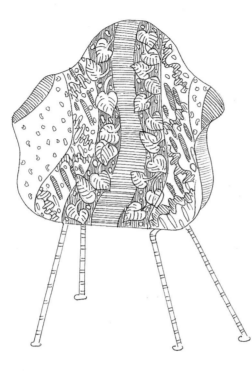

Charles Eames had many imitators, so finding fiberglass replicas of his most popular chair design should not be difficult. This armchair version, with an abundance of smooth surface, lends itself to decorative painting. A side view, showing both front and back surfaces, invites contrasting treatments. The front features two panels of philodendron vines with showy leaves and a black and dotted background. This pattern repeats on the arms.

An irregular combed pattern on the center panel separates the vines and reappears on the armrests. Combing resembles Colour Shaping in that you use a special tool to remove wet glaze from a varnished surface, revealing the color beneath. Panels of an abstract vine and raindrop pattern complete the front design. With so much area to cover and so rich an interaction among the bands of pattern, you will certainly want to prepare a detailed sketch. Your decor may not support so many patterns. If so, the combing or azure dots on black, alone, would be stunning.

Simple brushstrokes combine with rich color to create beautiful patterns.

The vine stems are curved strokes done with a script liner. The elongated raindrop pattern calls for exerting varying pressure with another script liner. The leaf shape, done with a flat shader, consists of two face-to-face comma strokes. Leaf veins are modified *S* strokes done with a script liner. A script liner also forms short raindrops, which are straight lines with pressure applied at the end of the stroke. For the small comma strokes, a script liner will work again. The combing tool produces the striped pattern in wet glaze over paint.

1 Choose the colors you would like to use on your chair and then paint swatches close to each other on palette paper. Red iron oxide is used for vine stems, black for raindrop shapes, apple green and leaf green for the leaves, blue-violet for raindrops, and azure for background and glaze.

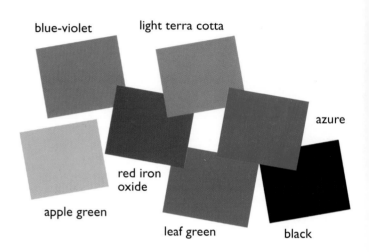

blue-violet   light terra cotta

azure

red iron oxide

apple green

leaf green   black

2 Prepare the surface, as described in Surface Preparation and Finishing. Using a 1" (or wider) brush and white latex paint, base-coat the front of the chair. Paint the back and legs azure. It makes economic sense to use latex paint from the hardware store to base-coat large areas. Sketch in "armrests" and a broad band down the middle of the chair. Using the 1" (2.5 cm) brush, paint these areas apple green. Then use a #4 flat shader or a #6 script liner to paint a blue-violet stripe on either side of the apple green band. After the paint is dry, use the 1" (2.5 cm) sponge brush to apply two coats of varnish.

3 Mix an azure glaze of one part paint and one part extender. Practice combing before working on the chair. Paint palette paper or Bristol board with the apple green color; after the paint is dry, apply two coats of varnish to seal in your work. When the varnish is thoroughly dry, use the 1" (2.5 cm) brush to apply a section of glaze about 4" (10 cm) wide. Press firmly as you rake the hard rubber combing tool across the glazed surface to create a crisp, striped pattern. Wipe the tool on a paper towel to remove excess glaze. When you feel confident in your skill, comb the broad apple green stripe and armrests. Varnish the combed sections.

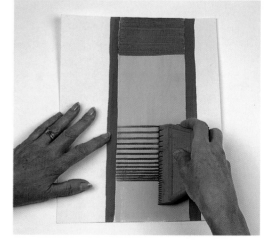

4 Make sure your patterns are well worked out on paper before starting on the chair. Use the quilter's pencil to outline broad bands on the chair as a guide to laying out the patterns. One band extends from the armrest to the area where the arms ease into the seat and back. The space between this arm area and the center combed band is about equally divided into two more bands. We will begin working from the center combed band out, on both sides, so sketch in the philodendron vine and background comma shapes onto both panels bordering the center section. Allow a few leaves and vine stems to extend over the central band.

5 Paint the leaves apple green with the #12 flat shader. For a smooth, free look, use pairs of large comma strokes to form the leaves, filling in as necessary. Use a #4 script liner and a modified *S* stroke to add leaf green veins to the leaves. Form vines by using the #4 script liner and red iron oxide to paint long curved strokes. You may want to try the panel patterns on paper or board before you work on the chair.

6 Use azure paint and the #6 script liner to paint commas in the shape of kidney beans. Then use a #4 flat shader to fill in the black background. Be sure to leave a little white showing around the vines and kidney beans to add contrast. While you are working with black paint, add short black lines with a #4 script liner to the blue-violet bands bordering the combed sections. Varnish each panel as you complete it to seal your work.

7 In the same way you sketched in the vines and kidney beans on the panels just completed, sketch in the ragged zigzag, raindrop, and kidney bean pattern on the panels to the left and right of the vine panels. Then paint the ragged zigzag in red iron oxide with a #8 flat shader. Try to keep the zigzag irregular and informal.

8 Using the #6 script liner, paint the raindrops, alternating between blue-violet and azure. To form the raindrops, pull the brush along and apply pressure as you end the stroke. Again, irregularity is a virtue. You will be adding more detail, but to be safe, seal in what you have done so far on the zigzag bands with a coat of varnish.

9 Add black kidney bean shapes, again with the #4 script liner. Then, use a #1 script liner to create an irregular, and finer, black raindrop pattern over the zigzags. These raindrops are just thin lines with occasional randomly applied pressure. Next, use a #4 script liner to fill in the background of the band with terra cotta. As before, leave some white as an accent. Varnish each panel as you complete it.

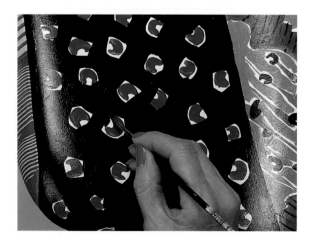

10 This step should be easy because you have done it before on the vine panels. Sketch, then paint, the same pattern of azure kidney beans and black background shown in step 5. You have created a masterpiece! Now finish the chair, as described in Surface Preparation and Finishing.

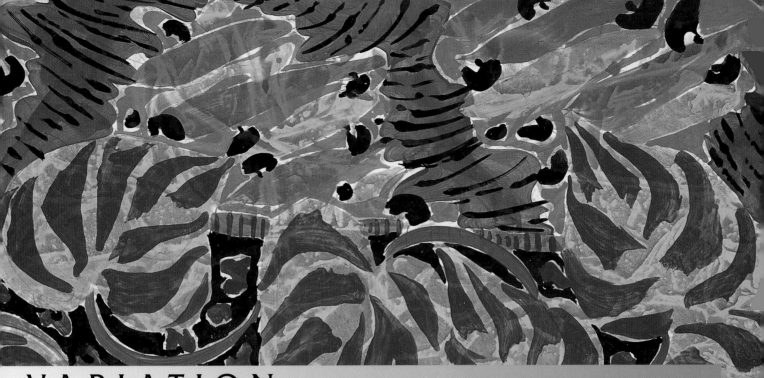

VARIATION: FUCHSIA PHILODENDRON

This variation begins with exactly the same design as the one you have already painted on the chair. To achieve even more of a jungle look, paint over the surface with a fuchsia glaze. Then create a texture with a stamp made of clear plastic wrap. See Batik Technique for details about creating this texture. Notice how the textured glaze makes the philodendron leaves even more tropical so that they resemble croton or caladium leaves. The glaze also intensifies other colors and transforms the white space.

OBJECT TIPS

You can easily find items for decorative painting at craft stores, but often the best places to get objects to decorate with colorful patterns are your own cellar, yard sales, flea markets, or thrift shops. At antique shops, ask to see damaged or imperfect antiques—the chair for this project was too stained to sell at premium prices.

MEXICAN MOTIF

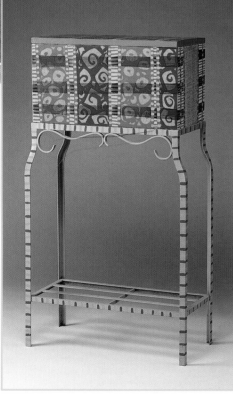

INSPIRATION *Memories of a trip to Mexico inspired this viv[id]
pattern. Travel offers new, visual worlds of artistic inspiration, and each geographic re[gion]
has its own characteristic style and palette: Think of the temperate
pastels of a Bermuda village; the misty grays, greens, and blues
of London along the Thames; or the gold, saffron, and scarlet
of a traditional temple in Thailand.*

This box in its wrought-iron stand triggered
images of the vivid natural colors and folk
art designs of Mexico and the Yucatan
coast. The artist adapted traditional
Mexican patterns produced by clay or
wooden stamps and used them as an
underlying design motif. Layered brushstrokes and glazes build surface decoration
that suits the shape of this chest, but
could easily be adapted to another
boxy shape. A bright palette of colors gives
the interpretation a contemporary look.

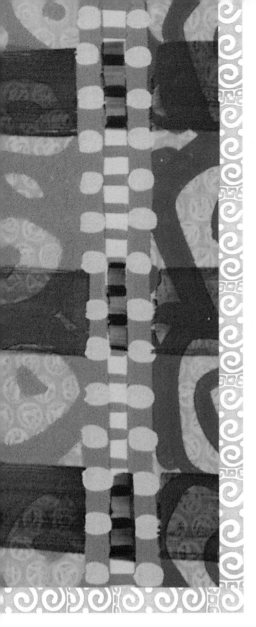

Make a simple sketch of the object you want to paint.

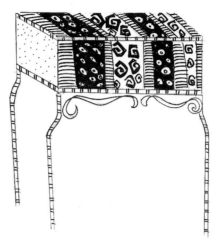

Although this pattern looks complicated, it is actually three simple brushstrokes over a base-coat stamped with bubble wrap for texture. The lines and smaller dots are painted with script-liner brushes, the largest dots are finger-painted thumbprints.

To begin, make a simple sketch of the object you want to paint. You may want to duplicate the sketch, so that you can try out several different design options. When choosing elements to combine into a pattern, first consider the large surfaces of the object and how often you want the pattern to repeat, then consider how the pattern will work—or can be adapted—for narrow areas such as legs and supports. Lay out your ideas on the sketch and adjust the proportions and position of the design. Unless you are a seasoned painter, it will help to make some full-size templates of the design elements. You can then transfer the basic shapes and elements to the surface with pencil or tracing paper as needed.

TOOLS AND MATERIALS

small chest or similar object that lends itself to large bands of color

brushes: a broad ³/4" (2 cm) brush; a #1, #4, and # 6 script-liner brush; a #4 flat brush; and a 1" (2.5 cm) sponge brush (or brushes that achieve similar effects)

primers: metal primer and sealer-primer

water-based flow acrylic paints: citrus green, olive green, lavender, blue-violet, peach, turquoise, terra cotta

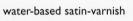

water-based satin-varnish

extender or plain water

bubble wrap

a drafting pencil or transfer paper

#600 superfine sandpaper

By combining simple brushstrokes, you can build an interesting, complex design

Use the # 4 script-liner brush to paint the narrow lines, and the #6 script-liner for the wide bands. To make the line less regular, as shown at far left, apply pressure as you paint. You can paint dots several ways: Use the wrong end of a brush or the tip of the #4 script-liner to paint small dots; use a #6 script-liner for larger dots; for still larger dots—dip your fingertip in the paint and touch the surface. Pressing down on the brush will make larger dots. Practice on paper before you start to paint.

1 On paper, paint samples of the colors you are considering. It may be helpful to use a color wheel to see relationships of contrast or harmony among the colors you select. Label the colors—base color, stripe color, dots, and so on—to avoid confusion when you begin to layer the pattern. Light, bright hues often work well as base colors, with more intense hues layered on top.

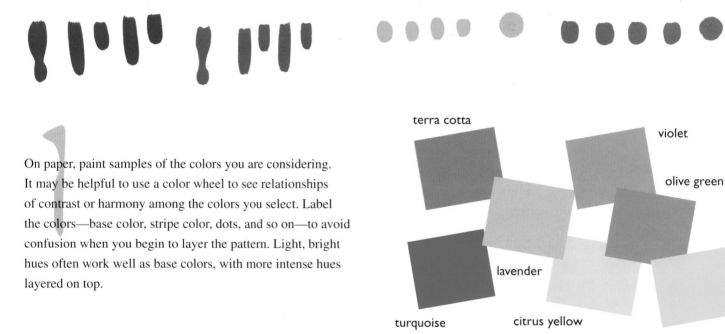

terra cotta

violet

olive green

lavender

turquoise

citrus yellow

peach

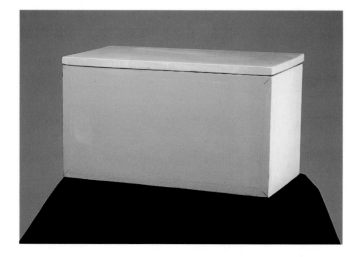

2 Paint the unfinished surface with a sealer-primer. If the surface is already sealed, remove any wax or dirt and test to make sure the paint sticks well. You may need to roughen the surface with sandpaper. Apply the base-coat color with a broad brush. In this case, the artist selected a light, bright citrus yellow to contrast with darker layers applied later.

GLAZE TIPS

Extender slows the drying time of paint. Water can substitute for extender, but the glaze consistency and drying time will be harder to control since water evaporates faster than extender. Even with added extender, paint may thicken if you are working for a long time—so be prepared to add more as you work.

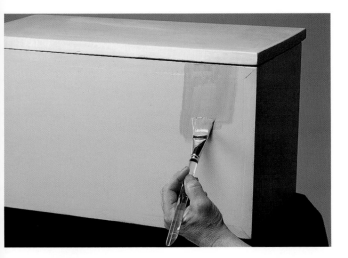

3 Prepare a glaze by mixing one part acrylic paint—here, olive green—with one part water-based extender. With the broad brush, apply the glaze in wide vertical stripes, one section at a time. Prepare to move quickly to the next step, before the glaze dries.

4 Place a strip of bubble wrap against the wet glaze. Since bubble wrap comes with air pockets in several sizes, you can get different effects, depending on the wrap you use. For a clean print, make sure all the pockets are filled with air. Press the bubble wrap gently and evenly into the glazed surface. You will see the texture developing through the clear plastic. Gently peel off the bubble wrap, being careful not to smudge the wet glaze. If you are satisfied, continue to the next section. If not, quickly rebrush the glaze and try again. Proceed one stripe at a time. When you have finished texturing, let the paint dry and then apply a coat of varnish.

5 Use a drafting pencil (or transfer paper if you are using a template) to sketch your pattern onto the prepared surface. Be careful not to press so firmly that you dent the surface of your piece. Here, the artist alternates curved and angular spiral design elements inspired by the Mexican print roller. You may wish to limit the design to one element, or you may choose a combination of elements.

Outline the design elements with the #1 script-liner, as shown. Then with a #4 flat brush, fill in the areas around the design motif. Alternate between lavender and blue-violet paint for each stripe—or choose a single color to define the entire motif. As you work, you may decide to leave other small areas exposed to define interesting shapes.

In the narrow gaps between stripes, use the #6 script-liner to embellish the design with "ladders" of thin vertical bands and horizontal brush strokes. Again, sketch the design in pencil if you need a guide. The vertical lines here are painted in lavender; the horizontal lines are terra cotta. Short, horizontal terra cotta stripes painted with a #4 script-liner make "steps" in the ladder. Last, use the #6 brush—or the tip of your finger—to overlay large peach dots on the lavender vertical stripe. Let dry and apply a coat of varnish to seal the design.

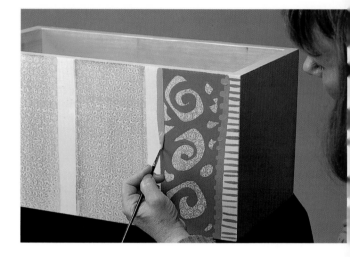

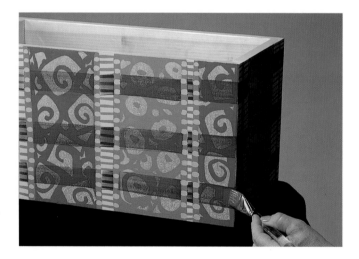

Before applying the glaze, make any final adjustments to the pattern. Mix one part turquoise acrylic paint with one part extender to make a glaze. Apply horizontal stripes of turquoise glaze with the ³/4" (2 cm) brush. The color of the glaze gives the overall pattern depth. If you paint a sample of the glaze on paper, you will see an amazing difference between the glaze alone and the glaze over the pattern. When you are satisfied with your creation, allow the print to dry, and varnish and sand following the instructions in Surface Preparation and Finishing.

BOX TIPS

You can use the techniques described so far on a box or another object without a stand of any kind. Even so, you may be wondering where you might find a box and stand if you wanted to reproduce this project exactly. The stand shown is an old aquarium stand found at a yard sale. A carpenter made the box to fit the stand. As an alternative, you might buy or make legs for any box or chest.

9 With the sponge brush, coat the stand with metal primer, let it dry, then apply a coat of pale lavender as a background color. You may also use traditional wrought-iron black. Varnish and let it dry.

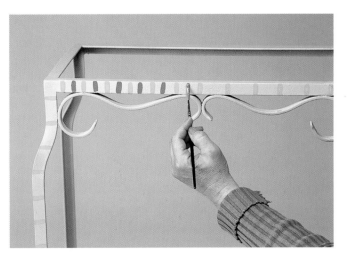

10 Approximately every inch (2.5 cm) or so, alternate stripes of citrus yellow paint with stripes of blue-violet. This links the stand with the box. Varnish and sand it, as described in Surface Preparation and Finishing.

VARIATION: FIESTA FLORAL

For an equally colorful but entirely different effect on a flat surface, you may want to try this layered plaid and floral pattern. The Mexican palette here is not cool but hot as a chili pepper. Dominant blue and orange—opposites on the color wheel—create vibrant visual excitement. Like the Mexican Motif, the plaid effect is created by overpainting a light, bright base-coat with glazes. The floral pattern is incised into the wet glaze with a Colour Shaper.

ENGLISH ROSES

INSPIRATION *When Gertrude Stein said, "A rose is a rose is a rose," she was talking about English roses. British gardens are famous for the lushness of their roses. Although horticulturists have produced many showy variations over the years, the old-fashioned blossoms with clusters of petals and subtle variations of color epitomize natural beauty. Many rose fanciers find the subtlest shades of pale pink, peach, and ivory the most appealing.*

It is no wonder that, over the years, many decorative painters have specialized in embellishing trays, boxes, and furniture with perfect roses, dewdrops and all. The roses that adorn this half-round table are freer than traditional painted roses. When you see the rose as a combination of simple brushstrokes, even a beginner can paint them with a little practice.

The simple patterns of stripes, checkerboard, and dots, complement the rose and leaf medallion.

It would be easy to overwhelm the delicate beauty of the roses in the medallion atop this half-round table. The simple patterns of stripes, checkerboard, and dots, however, complement the rose and leaf medallion rather than compete with it.

Similar tables are easy to find at reasonable prices. If you cannot find one, another table, a box, a bureau, or even a tray would look splendid decorated with some or all of these design elements. Whatever your object, begin by making a sketch and laying out the patterns you have chosen. Because the medallion area is a central focus, making a newsprint template to define the area for the rose and leaf pattern may be critical. The base coating, spattering, striping, checker-boarding, and dotting are easy to execute, so you can give full attention to the rose medallion.

TOOLS AND MATERIALS

half-round table or other object large enough to accommodate this combination of colors and patterns

brushes: a broad brush, approximately 1" (2.5 cm); #4 and #6 script liners; #4, #8, and #12 flat shaders; and a 1" (2.5 cm) sponge brush (or brushes that achieve similar effects)

toothbrush

sealer-primer

water-based flow acrylic paints: light violet, straw, light coral, mint green, dusty plum, leaf green, periwinkle blue, dark coral, light peach, light blue, and black

water-based varnish

sandpaper: medium grade (#150 or #400) and #600 superfine

quilter's pencil

newspaper, shelf paper, or other paper for making a template

The rose form is a deceptively uncomplicated design element.

Its petals are nothing more than large, free, rose-colored comma strokes executed with a flat shader. Short, square, mint green strokes created with another flat shader build the checkerboard. The border of large black dots and smaller light violet dots is painted with a script liner.

1 To prevent a color conflict among the many colors used, we selected a subdued palette with muted hues. None of the stronger colors—straw, leaf green, periwinkle blue, or dark coral—could be considered strident or overpowering. Paint examples of the colors you have selected onto a paper palette.

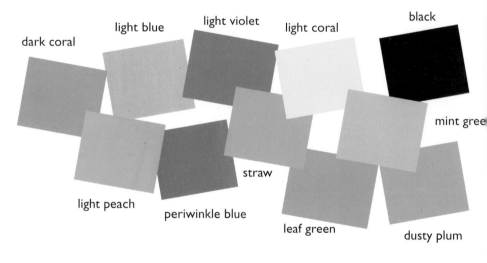

dark coral   light blue   light violet   light coral   black

light peach   periwinkle blue   straw   leaf green   mint gree   dusty plum

2 Prepare the surface, as described in Surface Preparation. Using a 1" (2.5 cm) brush and light peach paint, apply a base coat to the entire piece. After the peach paint dries and using the same brush, apply a light blue band to the table lip and paint the upper knob and feet of the legs light blue. Add a band of light coral at the lower ridge of the table apron. Make short, rectangular strokes in the same color with a #4 flat shader to create a crenelation above the light coral band. Again using the 1" (2.5 cm) brush, paint the middle knobs of the legs straw. Wait for the paint to dry and varnish the entire piece to seal your work so far.

3 Using black paint, lightly spatter the entire piece, except the top. To spatter, dip a toothbrush in black paint diluted with an equal part of water. Hold the toothbrush in one hand. Pull the index finger of the other hand across the brush to spray tiny specks of paint onto the surface. This method allows maximum control of the size and density of the spatter. Practice on paper before spattering your piece. Wait for the paint to dry and varnish the spattered surfaces.

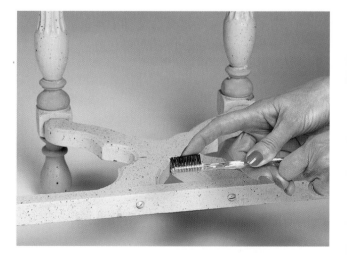

Create a full-size template of the medallion by cutting a piece of newsprint or other paper to form a large semicircle. Fold the semicircle in half and cut a scalloped edge. The medallion covers approximately two-thirds of the tabletop area. Then, using the template as a pattern, outline the scalloped semicircle on the tabletop with the quilter's pencil.

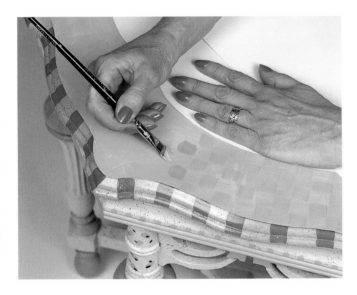

Use straw paint and the 1" (2.5 cm) brush to paint the area outside the medallion. Let the paint dry and then add the checkerboard pattern with a #12 flat shader. This can be done freehand, but be sure to keep the strokes evenly spaced. Start at the outside edge and work toward the medallion. After the paint has dried, varnish the medallion.

Sketch the floral pattern in the medallion with the quilter's pencil. This can be done freehand or you could make a full-size sketch and trace the design onto the table. Begin painting the roses. Use the #8 flat shader to form large, free, comma strokes in light coral. You could outline the petal with a smaller brush and fill in the shape, but you will sacrifice spontaneity. Refer to the tip box for more information on making roses with the comma stroke. Practice on paper before you paint on the table.

7 Use the #6 script liner to add finer comma-shaped petals in deep coral to form the roses. Use the same technique of applying and releasing pressure to achieve a free comma shape. After a little practice, you will be amazed at the beautiful impressionistic rose forms you can create. After the paint has dried, protect your roses with a coat of varnish.

8 Apply a base coat of dusty plum for the leaf shapes between the roses, using a #12 flat shader. If you like, allow the leaves to spill outside the border of the medallion. Then use a #4 script liner to add leaf green veins to the leaves. These can be free and irregular shapes rather than smooth lines.

9 Use the #6 script liner and light violet paint to fill in most of the background. Be sure to leave some light peach base coat showing to fully form the roses. Allow the violet paint to dry thoroughly. Use the same size brush to add small irregular mint green shapes among the roses and leaves. Varnish the medallion after all the paint has dried.

COMMA-STROKE ROSE TIPS

Load the #8 flat shader with paint. Hold the brush at a 45 degree angle to the surface and apply pressure as you touch the flat edge of the brush to the surface. Slowly release the pressure as you move the brush in a curved, comma shape. Try to remain loose and free, without losing control.

10 Using a #4 script liner and periwinkle blue, paint small circles randomly between the roses and leaves on top of the light violet, mint green, and light peach background. Allow the paint to dry. Use the same brush and black paint to add small *V* shapes. Try to avoid covering the roses or leaves.

11 Add a band of black dots formed with a #6 script liner around the edge of the medallion scallop. Then, when the black paint is thoroughly dry, add off-center light violet dots with the #4 script liner. If you prefer, use other dot-making tools, such as the tip of your finger or the wrong end of the brush.

12 Add periwinkle blue stripes over the light blue lip of the table, using the #12 flat shader. With the #6 script liner, add mint green stripes to the upper light blue knobs of the table legs. Add random straw dots to the upper table legs, using the #6 script liner or your fingertip. Wait for the straw paint to dry before you add small black dots with the #4 script liner or with the wrong end of the brush. Finish the table, following the instructions in Surface Preparation and Finishing.

VARIATION: FLASHY ROSES

The variation also features roses. The palette is slightly different, employing more vibrant colors. Impressionistic strawberries replace the leaf forms. Cross-hatching, square dots, and other random shapes fill the background.

CRAZY QUILT

INSPIRATION *From the late 1850s through the early part of the twentieth century, women stitched traditional quilts for use in the privacy of the bedroom but created crazy quilts "for show" in their best parlor. Traditional quilts usually consisted of pieces of cotton or linen fabrics, often in subdued colors, cut into geometric shapes and sewn together to form precise patterns. In contrast, crazy quilts often featured brightly colored, irregular-shaped pieces in more extravagant fabrics—velvet, satin, brocade, taffeta. Sometimes quilts were made of scraps from favorite gowns. Embroidery often accented segments of the quilt.*

A hexagonal plant stand often stood in the same parlor as the quilt, usually topped by a Boston fern. We have adapted the crazy quilt characteristics of sharp angles and eclectic patterns and applied it to the plant stand. Irregular spiky sections divide the top of the plant stand. Each segment displays a different painted pattern.

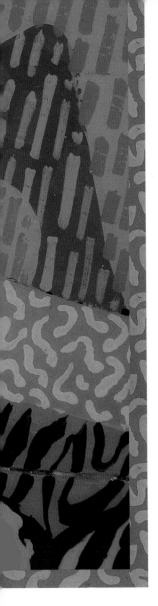

Try using the same pattern on a small table, box, or tray.

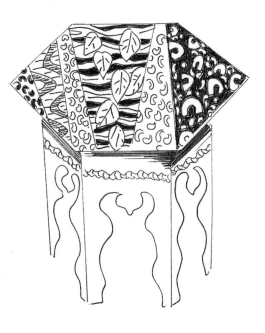

You can often find similar, inexpensive plant stands made of pine or oak in used furniture stores, country auctions, or flea markets. Stay away from the fancier (and pricier) stands found in antique stores. These are too valuable to paint and should be left as is to protect their value. If you can't find a stand, try using the same pattern on a small table, box, or tray.

Begin by making a sketch and defining the sections you will paint with each pattern. You could reinterpret the patterns in colors other than the ones shown to coordinate with your decor or simplify the design by using only one or two patterns divided by segments of plain unpatterned color.

A stamp made of clear plastic wrap produces a batik-like texture on the base in two color schemes: teal over apricot on the lower base; terra cotta over apricot on the upper base. A band of light violet beads separates the two halves of the base, and teal stripes enhance the lip of the tabletop. The colors found in the base also occur on the tabletop to unite the piece.

TOOLS AND MATERIALS

wooden plant stand or other object large enough to accommodate this combination of colors and patterns

brushes: a broad brush, approximately 1" (2.5 cm); #1, #2, and #4 script liners; #4 and #12 flat shaders; and a 1" (2.5 cm) sponge brush (or brushes that achieve similar effects)

sealer-primer

water-based flow acrylic paints: goldenrod, violet, apricot, teal, light olive, black, terra cotta, light violet, and eggplant

water-based varnish

sandpaper: medium grade (#150 or #400) and #600 superfine

extender or blending medium

clear plastic wrap

quilter's or drawing pencil

newspaper or paper towels

Colour Shaper (for variation)

Simple brushstrokes are the key to success with this project.

The tabletop patterns use several interesting, but simple, brushstrokes. The short curved shapes and the goldenrod stripes are formed with a script liner. Shape the leaf form by applying and releasing pressure with a flat shader. The veins of the leaf are just irregular lines formed with a script liner. The black wood grain pattern is formed with irregular lines and a script liner.

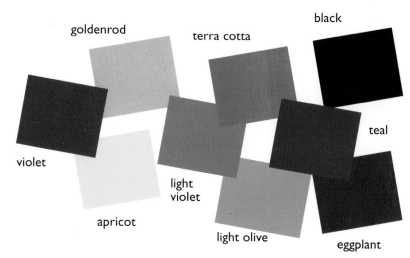

goldenrod

terra cotta

black

violet

teal

light violet

apricot

light olive

eggplant

1 The patterns shown on the tabletop resemble fabric designs employing many colors. Despite this variety, the colors coordinate well together. Whatever your personal color choices, prepare a palette by painting small swatches of each color onto a piece of paper.

2 Prepare the surface as instructed in Surface Preparation and Finishing. Using a 1" (2.5 cm) brush and apricot paint, apply a base coat to the entire piece. Allow the paint to dry, then use the #4 script liner (or a smaller brush, if you prefer) to paint the light violet beads that divide the top and bottom of the base. Use the #4 script liner to paint narrow teal stripes around the edge of the tabletop. You could save the beading and striping for last, but notice how attractively these colors work together.

3 Prepare a sketch of the table, including the layout of the pattern. Using your sketch as a guide, divide the tabletop into five geometric panels with your quilter's pencil. Leave the outside panels apricot. Paint the remaining panels terra cotta, light violet, and goldenrod. Use a 1" (2.5 cm) brush or larger. Allow the paint to dry thoroughly. Apply two coats of varnish with the 1" (2.5 cm) foam brush to protect your work and provide a base for additional work.

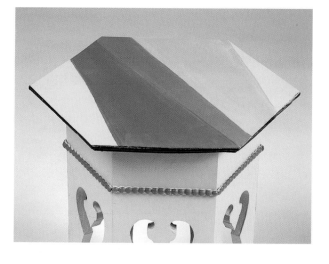

4 Using a quilter's or drawing pencil, sketch the wide arch and dot pattern on one apricot section of the tabletop. You will probably be able to do this freehand, but you could make a full-size template and trace the design, if you prefer. Using the #4 script liner and eggplant paint, fill in the background around the arches. Wait for the paint to dry, then varnish this section.

5 With the #1 script liner, paint small, curved, comma-like light violet shapes onto the eggplant background. After a little practice on paper, this can easily be done freehand. Arrange the shapes randomly, but avoid the temptation to paint them in lines. Instead nest the shapes into each other. Allow the paint to dry and varnish this section.

6 With a pencil, draw large leaf shapes onto the terra cotta section. Use the #12 flat shader to paint the leaves in teal. This is a good opportunity to practice using a pair of comma strokes to form the leaf, or you can simply outline and fill in the leaf. After the teal paint dries, varnish the leaves in case you need to make corrections in the next step.

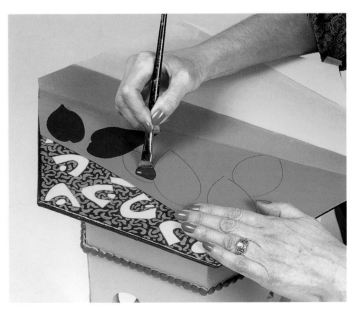

Add light olive veins to the leaves with the #4 script liner. Use modified *S* strokes to create a free feeling. Then, using the #2 script liner, add an irregular wood grain pattern to the terra cotta background. To produce the simple, textured effect, follow the pattern in the photo or the grain pattern from a wooden object. Again, this can probably be done freehand but could be sketched in first as a guide to painting. Allow to dry, then varnish this section.

Use the #1 script liner to add small, apricot comma shapes to the light violet section. Allow the paint to dry. Using the same script liner, add teal comma shapes to the remaining apricot band. As before, keep the shapes random and nested, rather than in lines. Varnish these sections after the paint dries.

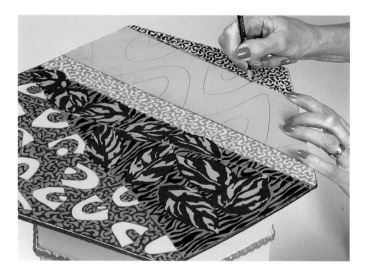

Using the drawing or quilter's pencil, sketch broad arch shapes on the goldenrod section. Try to keep the arches evenly spaced. Notice how the negative space, which is the background, forms a pattern, as well. If you prefer a more geometric pattern, you could use broad, parallel zigzag bands instead.

VARNISH TIPS

It is wise to varnish between steps whenever you are working with a layered pattern. This seals the work beneath and protects it so later mistakes or changes can be removed back to the varnish. Varnish also provides an essential base for glazing and texturing. When working in sections, you should not only allow the paint to dry and varnish between steps, but also seal in each section with a coat of varnish as you finish painting it. This assures that you will not accidentally damage your work when you move on to another section.

Paint the arches eggplant with the #12 flat shader. To be safe, varnish this section after it dries and before adding design details. When the varnish is dry, add light olive dashes over the arches and terra cotta dashes over the goldenrod background. These dashes can easily be done freehand, but if you worry about keeping the lines parallel, you could sketch them lightly with a quilter's pencil. Let dry and varnish the entire table top.

Mix a teal glaze of one part paint and one part extender. Apply the glaze to one section of the stand. Make a stamp by loosely wrapping a strip of clear plastic wrap around your fingers. (See Batik Technique for photos of this process.) Then press the stamp onto the base below the light violet beads to create a batik texture. Blot the excess glaze on newspaper or paper towels. Repeat this process, using a clean stamp and terra cotta glaze on the base above the light violet beads. Follow the finish procedures described at the beginning of the book in Surface Preparation and Finishing.

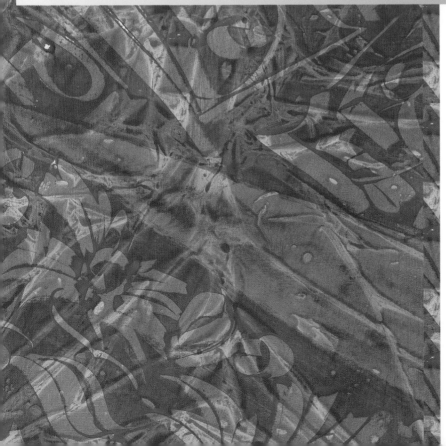

VARIATION: FLORAL CRAZY QUILT

The Floral Crazy Quilt pattern uses the same angular geometric layout, but it is achieved in a different way. Begin with a yellow base coat and then two coats of varnish. Mix a turquoise glaze and use a clear plastic wrap stamp to texture the surface. Let dry and apply varnish. Mix a rust glaze and apply it to angular geometric sections, leaving one or more sections of turquoise texture unglazed. With a Colour Shaper, incise the floral pattern into the rust glaze. Prepare a blue-violet glaze and apply it over the teal textured panels. Finish as described in Surface Preparation and Finishing.

Creative Uses

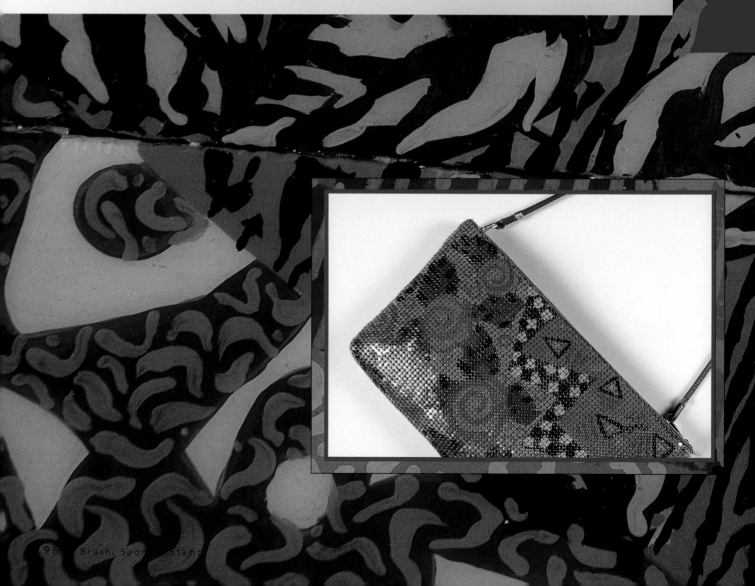

Creative Uses
FOR THE HOME

If you have completed one or more of the projects in the preceding chapters, you have experienced the intense satisfaction of creating useful art. The demonstrated patterns and techniques, including variations for each project, along with the final section, detailing how to create twenty more patterns, provide you with a portfolio of glorious decorative options. Along the way, you may have experimented with adaptations or interpretations of your own.

You have seen how a variety of sources of creative inspiration have developed into finished projects. You have learned how to develop motifs and patterns and how to sketch your ideas. You have laid out fabulous palettes and mixed glazes and washes. You have learned to execute basic brushstrokes and seen how the simplest brush technique can create impressive results. And you know how to prepare a surface for painting and, when your work is done, to build a museum-quality finish to enhance and preserve your work. This is just the beginning.

You are now prepared to apply your new accomplishments to enhance your home in any number of ways. Once again, the creative process comes into play. Looking through your artist's eyes, you will see intriguing color combinations and fascinating textures. You will automatically begin figuring out how to reproduce or adapt them. You will also see the objects and surfaces around you in a new way: not just as background, but as opportunities to apply your art. For example, how can you use the decorative elements in that drapery pattern to pull the room together?

In fact, it is easy to get carried away. The husband of one new decorative artist exclaimed, "Honey, this is great, but are you going to paint everything?" For most people, time will be the only limitation to what you can do. In the next few pages, we present a range of ideas for the home. Again, you may borrow these ideas or use them as a springboard for your own creativity.

Fabric painting and stamping techniques can easily be applied to create unique pillows to add pizzazz to your parlor. This example employs the stamping and wash procedures you learned in the textiles section.

When your window treatment calls for a special something, consider these ball and tassel accessories to enhance your draperies. The wooden balls with a hole drilled through can be painted to match your decor. Then pull a tassel through the hole to attach to your rod.

You may find interestingly shaped wooden bowls at flea markets or yard sales. Usually, a rough sanding will create a paintable surface. Notice how two patterns, one on the interior and one on the exterior, add interest.

Look around your home. Would an interesting texture and stamped pattern save that old end table from storage in the attic? Could decorative ornaments spruce up your old window treatment? With a little time and a few layers of paint and glaze, the unfinished bowl or pitcher you found at the craft store could become a focal point for your cupboard. Use this section as a resource for ideas to apply your decorative skills in your own surroundings.

A gaily decorated wooden pitcher can light up your sideboard. Because working a brush inside the pitcher may pose a problem, consider using spray paint and varnish to cover the interior.

A board painted in any pattern you like forms a dazzling background to a round mirror applied with a glue gun and trimmed with beading. You could also decorate a plain picture frame and insert a mirror.

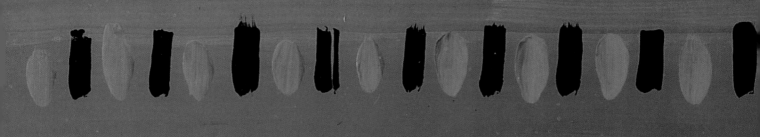

Creative Uses
FOR GIFTS

Ivory-tower artists may proclaim that they create art for its own sake, not to please others. Decorative artists, on the other hand, generally believe that art is elevated when it pleases not only the artist, but others. Since gift-giving opportunities abound, you will, no doubt, find countless opportunities to please others with unique and thoughtful presents. Of course, any of the projects described in earlier chapters would be splendid gifts. Wouldn't your sister love a lamp that adds a stylish accent to her new home office? Or could those special newlyweds use a decorated chair to fill one of the spaces in their sparsely furnished apartment?

More often, however, you may want to create thoughtful, but less complex, tokens of your affection and friendship, such as a painted purse or tote bag, hand-decorated jewelry, or paperware. Any gift becomes special when packaged in hand-painted boxes or printed gift wrap. One new decorative painter practiced her first pattern on old cookie tins. Then she stocked the tins with needles, pins, scissors, a tape measure, and other sewing items to give as gifts to her grown children, out on their own for the first time. The same tins filled with food goodies would make a great hostess gift or a cheerful item to take to an ailing senior citizen.

All the gifts shown are small in scale and therefore reasonably quick and easy to execute. Some are made of the leftovers from other projects. Why should you throw away the trimmed edge of a beautifully painted floor cloth or the samples you painstakingly developed on Bristol board? Waste not, want not. With a little time and ingenuity, you can use the techniques you have learned to delight your family and friends with special gifts.

Although you can purchase items to decorate as presents for your friends and family, most of the gifts shown involve recycling, refurbishing, or enhancing small everyday items or accessories. Most of the techniques are relatively easy to complete in less than an hour. You may create special items for special people, or you may have so much fun painting, sponging, and stamping that you find you have created a small cache of gifts, ready for the next gift-giving occasion.

A small, metal link shoulder bag becomes an unusual evening accessory for a special friend when decorated with painted roses and other simple design elements. No boutique could do better.

A teen-aged artist produces fancy footwear for her friends. It started when a pair of her own favorite scuffs began looking worn. Sneakers are other candidates for decorative patterns.

Practice patterns on Bristol board can be cut into small shapes to create vibrant contemporary pins and earrings. The pins and earrings can be finished with multiple coats of varnish or coated with a pour-on, high-gloss finish.

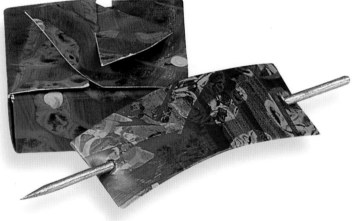

Practice patterns on Bristol board become nifty gift containers. Paint each side of the Bristol board a different pattern or texture. Then cut box shapes using an Origami pattern, score fold lines with a blunt tool, and presto—special packaging.

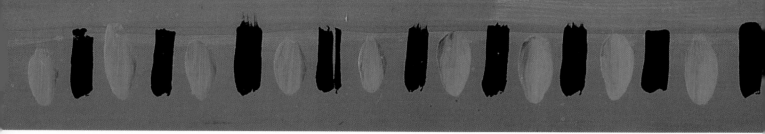

Painted and textured paper becomes a snappy cover for a standard address book. This can either be glued to the book or folded and taped to form a removable cover like the ones you made for your school books.

Scraps left over from trimming placemats or floor cloths can be cut into strips to make handsome book marks. Alternatively, designs on Bristol board can serve the same purpose.

Make your own stamped, painted, or textured gift wrap in minutes out of shelf or other plain paper. Use any pattern that does not require many layers of paint or glaze, as many layers will make the paper too stiff to fold neatly.

Unique stationery and calling cards for personal or professional use feature a simple textured border. The same approach could be applied to print note cards. Stamped designs are also effective to create individualized correspondence papers.

Color Inspirations

The inspiration for the patterns in each project shown in this book came from a different source: one from a quilt, one from a Mexican folk art stamp, one from a rose garden, and so on. Sources of color inspiration are just as varied. In fact, color inspirations are all around you, limited only by your ability to see the world in a new way—through the eyes of the artist in you. The next few pages provide examples of palettes that may be derived from specific examples of nature, textiles, china, and fine art.

Look around your home. What are your favorite possessions or furnishings? What colors create the effect you admire? Study your favorite print dress or patterned sweater. What colors combine to form the design? Which store windows catch your eye? Do you see a similar array of colors in all these places? If so, you may have a clearly preferred personal palette. That's certainly a good base to work from. In your sketch book, paint small swatches of these colors and note how they work together.

As you rest in a garden, stroll through a park, or hike through a forest, squint your eyes. Look at a single flower or a field of them. What colors do you see? Nature is a great color mixer. Again, make color notes in your sketch book of color combinations you'd like to try.

Visit a museum, paying less attention to the subject matter than to the colors of great paintings. Examine historical tapestries and textiles with special attention to the use of color. Do quick color sketches for later reference. Of course, the work of other decorative painters will give you lots of ideas, and pattern books abound. See "Resources" for a list of helpful titles.

In the classic film *The Wizard of OZ*, a tornado transports the heroine, Dorothy, from her home in black and white Kansas to the magical Technicolor land of OZ. When you awaken to the world of color around you, as Dorothy did, new adventures and excitement are sure to follow.

CHINA

Hand-painted china has long been a treasured form of decorative painting. The variety in color and pattern is mind-boggling. Most of us can select only one china pattern. Fortunately, as an artist, you can choose many patterns as color inspiration. You may have a pattern you love in your own cabinet.

Museums often show fine china. Alternatively, visit antique shops that carry dinnerware to see numbers of the fine old patterns. You will find contemporary patterns in department and specialty stores. Look to ceramics and pottery for more special color ideas.

These examples of fine Dresden china were hand painted in the late 1800s. The delicate floral patterns are executed in colors and tints of the same colors. Tints are colors lightened by adding white. The artist underpainted aster and rose forms in tints of magenta, violet, and burnt orange and then added details in the more intense pure colors. Tints of yellow and blue create subtle contrast. Leaf forms are avocado and a light tint of avocado. Delicate gold trim enhances the floral pattern. Generally, using tints of stronger colors assures harmony but can appear bland. Notice how the unlikely combination of magenta, violet, and orange creates a bright, vibrant visual dance of the flowers.

NATURE

Artists from time immemorial have turned to nature as a source of inspiration. As the impressionists have demonstrated so vividly, unlikely colors combine in nature to create the beautiful scenes and objects we admire. The sea is not just blue and green but may have highlights of lavender or coral. An oriental poppy is a glorious crimson but, when you look carefully, you also see pale green, eggplant, golden yellow, and lavender.

The illustration shows a collection of leaves and berries gathered on a crisp autumn afternoon. The larger leaves had fallen from a giant oak. The smaller were plucked from an ampelopsis vine. The ampelopsis also produces unimpressive flowers, followed by brilliant lapis berries.

Even this small sample of leaves and berries suggests a rich palette: The oak leaves and stems display subdued colors—light brown and dark brown—as well as warmer hues, such as straw, red iron oxide, and terra cotta. The ampelopsis leaves are bright yellow-green and citrus yellow. The predominant color of the berries is a deep lapis blue.

Like Mother Nature you might use all of these colors for a project, or you might select a narrower palette—for example, the colors of the oak leaves alone or the colors of the ampelopsis leaves and berries, accented with white and black. Either of these would create a different but pleasing effect.

FINE ART

Fine art in any medium can provide a rich source of color inspiration. Don't feel guilty. Replicating or adapting the color scheme of a masterpiece is not cheating. Artists have always learned by copying great examples. Stroll around a museum or art gallery. Squint your eyes. Pay attention to th color scheme, rather than the subject. When you see color combinations that appeal to you, stop and take notes either indicating color names, or better yet, rendering in colored pencil. Many museums require special permission to use paints or pastels.

The contemporary Chinese artist Huang Xuanzhi uses the traditional *shuiyin* (water-based printing) process to achieve subtle variations of color. In this print, entitled "After Rain," the basic palette is largely monochromatic. Jade green and a lighter tint of jade dominate the leaves, with veins outlined in a dark teal. Lotus flowers use this same pale jade green, along with light blue over snowy white. Red iron oxide and a lighter tint of this red define and set off the carp. The same tint of red iron oxide is repeated in the lotus flower centers, along with lemon yellow. Black water swirls over a deep gray-blue undercurrent. White rain drops on the lotus leaves remind us of the rain that has just fallen.

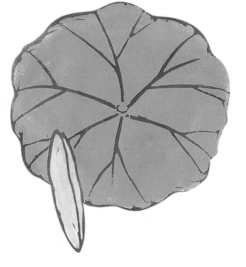

TEXTILES

Textile designers and needlework artists "paint" with dye
and thread. You can look for color ideas in a fabric shop, in
the textile collection of a museum, or in your own closet. It
is easier to see the colors in textiles because part of the
production process involves color separation. Sometimes,
each color used in a fabric is printed in a series of little
squares on the selvages. If so, you have an automatic palette.

If you look closely, you can single out individual threads in needlework. In fact, needle workers often array the threads they will use on a tool that closely resembles an artist's palette. Pattern books for embroidery, crewel work, quilting, and knitting can also be sources of color inspiration.

The rich handmade textile shown is the back of a jacket that was created from pieces of antique Middle-Eastern embroidery and beadwork. The desired effect here is brilliance and diversity of color. Light turquoise, turquoise, light jade green, periwinkle blue, violet, pale peach, tangerine, scarlet, maroon, and magenta are only some of the colors in this intricate pattern, accented with gold and silver metallic thread and beads and sequins of many colors. The black embroidery both defines patterns and separates colors that might otherwise clash, much like the lead outlining in a stained glass window.

Library of Patterns

You can find patterns in strange places. Look under your rug. You may find a rubber or plastic liner used to keep the rug from slipping. You probably don't want to cut this up, although some eager artists have!

To create this pattern, you will need:

a large textured carpet liner, as pictured

a broad brush

water-based extenders

clear plastic wrap (optional)

light green and blue-green flow acrylic paints

water-based varnish

1 Apply the light green base coat color and let dry. Apply a coat of water-based varnish over the base coat and let dry. Cut a strip of carpet liner about 4" x 12" (10 cm x 30 cm) and use it to practice step 2; when you master the technique, cut a piece to suit the size of your project.

2 Mix a glaze using one part blue-green acrylic paint and one part extender. Apply the blue-green glaze to the surface with a broad brush. Press the carpet liner smoothly and evenly into the wet glaze. To avoid getting paint on your hands, you may wish to place a layer of plastic film over the carpet liner before applying pressure. You will probably see some of the glaze seeping through the holes.

3 Press down with your hands or a flat object, such as a book. Peel back a corner of the carpet liner to make sure the pattern is coming through. If not, press harder. Peel off the carpet liner.

4 If the pattern is not what you want, quickly reglaze and try again. Be careful not to apply the glaze too thickly or let it dry out before printing with the liner.

Not all carpet liners are the same. In addition to the more common fine-textured ones, there are several in larger checked or waffle patterns. This creates opportunities for variation. When you are out shopping, keep your eyes out for new, interesting liner textures.

To create this pattern, you will need:

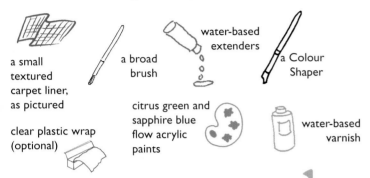

a small textured carpet liner, as pictured

clear plastic wrap (optional)

a broad brush

water-based extenders

citrus green and sapphire blue flow acrylic paints

a Colour Shaper

water-based varnish

1 Apply the citrus green base coat color and let dry. Apply a coat of water-based varnish over the base coat and let dry. Cut a strip of carpet liner about 4" x 12" (10 cm x 30 cm) and use it to practice step 2; when you master the technique, cut a piece to suit the size of your project.

2 Mix a glaze using one part sapphire blue acrylic paint and one part extender. Apply the sapphire blue glaze to the surface with a broad brush. Press the carpet liner smoothly and evenly into the wet glaze. You will probably see some of the glaze seeping through the holes. To avoid getting paint on your hands, you may wish to place a layer of plastic film over the carpet liner before applying pressure.

3 Press down with your hands or a flat object, such as a book. Peel back a corner of the carpet liner to make sure the pattern is coming through. If not, press harder. Peel off the carpet liner.

4 If the pattern is not what you want, quickly reglaze and try again. Be careful not to apply the glaze too thickly or let it dry out before printing with the liner.

5 Mix and apply a glaze of a third color right over the texture already created. Use the Colour Shaper to incise lines or shapes to form a design or pattern. Our example shows a simple zigzag border and a freehand floral pattern, but experiment to create designs and patterns of your own. As one artist commented, "It's like finger painting without the mess!"

The patterns on these facing pages are textured with bubble wrap. Bubble wrap is a plastic product covered with round air pockets and is used to protect breakable items during shipping. The next time you receive a package containing bubble wrap, save it for a decorating project.

To create this pattern, you will need:

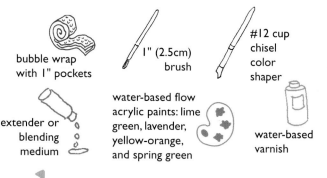

bubble wrap with 1" pockets

1" (2.5cm) brush

#12 cup chisel color shaper

extender or blending medium

water-based flow acrylic paints: lime green, lavender, yellow-orange, and spring green

water-based varnish

1 Use the 1" (2.5 cm) brush to apply a lime green base coat and let it dry. Apply two coats of varnish to form a slick surface. When the varnish is dry, mix a lavender glaze made of one part lavender paint and one part extender.

2 Cut bubble wrap to the appropriate size. Check to see that no bubbles are broken; broken bubbles will not print well. Use the 1" (2.5 cm) brush to apply lavender glaze evenly over the lime green base coat. Press the bubble wrap down firmly into the glazed surface. You will see the glaze crinkling in each bubble. Peel the bubble wrap off slowly.

3 Prepare a yellow-orange glaze by mixing one part extender with one part paint. Use the 1" (2.5 cm) brush to paint regular stripes over the bubble-wrap-textured surface. Notice how the color changes. Apply two coats of varnish.

4 When the varnish is dry, prepare a spring green glaze by mixing one part paint with one part extender. Working one section at a time, apply the spring green glaze. Use the #12 cup chisel color shaper to remove glaze to form the sun and Japanese character motifs. Continue working one section at a time. Varnish to protect your work.

As on the previous page, the color shaper and the hard rubber comb add designs over the bubble-wrap texture. Both the color shaper and the comb remove glaze, but each produces a very different effect.

To create this pattern, you will need:

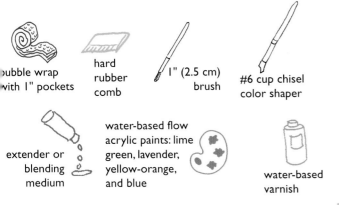

bubble wrap with 1" pockets

hard rubber comb

1" (2.5 cm) brush

#6 cup chisel color shaper

extender or blending medium

water-based flow acrylic paints: lime green, lavender, yellow-orange, and blue

water-based varnish

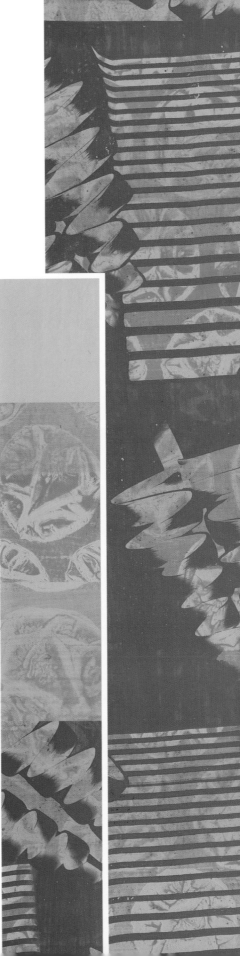

1 Use the 1" (2.5 cm) brush to apply a lime green base coat and let dry. Apply two coats of varnish to form a slick surface. When the varnish is dry, mix a lavender glaze made of one part lavender paint and one part extender.

2 Cut bubble wrap to the appropriate size. Check to see that no bubbles are broken; broken bubbles will not print well. Use the 1" (2.5 cm) brush to apply the lavender glaze evenly over the lime green base coat. Press the bubble wrap down firmly into the glazed surface. You will see the glaze crinkling in each bubble. Peel the bubble wrap off slowly.

3 Prepare a yellow-orange glaze by mixing one part extender with one part paint. Use the 1" (2.5 cm) brush to paint regular stripes over the bubble-wrap-textured surface. Notice how the color changes. Apply two coats of varnish.

4 When the varnish is dry, prepare a blue glaze by mixing one part paint with one part extender. Working one section at a time, apply the blue glaze. Comb rectangular sections. Then, working quickly, use the #6 cup chisel color shaper to remove glaze to form the pine tree motifs. Allow the trees to overlap the combed section. Glaze another section and repeat. Varnish to protect your work.

In the previous pattern, the hard rubber comb produced rectangles. In this pattern, long, vertical combed strokes form an irregular grill. The Colour Shaper creates a second, scroll motif.

To create this pattern, you will need:

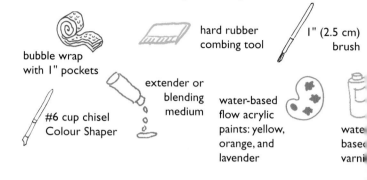

bubble wrap
with 1" pockets

hard rubber
combing tool

1" (2.5 cm)
brush

#6 cup chisel
Colour Shaper

extender or
blending
medium

water-based
flow acrylic
paints: yellow,
orange, and
lavender

wate
based
varni

Use the 1" (2.5 cm) brush to apply a yellow base coat and let dry. Apply two coats of varnish to form a slick surface. When the varnish is dry, mix an orange glaze made of one part paint and one part extender.

Cut bubble wrap to the appropriate size. Check to see that no bubbles are broken; broken bubbles will not print well. Use the 1" (2.5 cm) brush to apply the orange glaze evenly over the yellow base coat. Press the bubble wrap down firmly into the glazed surface. You will see the glaze crinkling in each bubble. Peel the bubble wrap off slowly. Apply two coats of varnish.

When the varnish is dry, prepare a lavender glaze by mixing one part paint with one part extender. Working one section at a time, apply the lavender glaze. Comb long vertical strokes to form a grill. Then, working quickly, use the #6 cup chisel Colour Shaper to remove glaze to form the scroll motifs right over the combed section. The scrolls are just fancy *S* strokes. Glaze another section and repeat. Varnish to protect your work.

Usually, you try to avoid runny paint. But when you mix a wash, you deliberately create a watery consistency so that it will run. The soft blended background underlies a bold pattern, outlined with a marker pen.

To create this pattern, you will need:

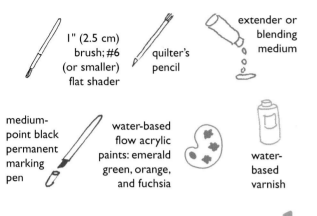

1" (2.5 cm) brush; #6 (or smaller) flat shader

quilter's pencil

extender or blending medium

medium-point black permanent marking pen

water-based flow acrylic paints: emerald green, orange, and fuchsia

water-based varnish

1
Prepare two washes, one green and one orange, by mixing one part paint with four parts water. Use the 1" (2.5 cm) brush to paint on the orange wash. Then create a pattern with the green wash by holding the brush almost perpendicular to the surface, then pressing down slightly and letting the green wash run into the orange wash. Move the brush and repeat to create diagonal stripes. You can also create texture by simply spattering a little green wash here and there.

2
With the quilter's pencil, sketch in space satellite shapes, circles with wedges taken out, crescents, full circles, or whatever shapes you like.

3
Prepare a fuchsia glaze by mixing one part paint with one part extender. With the #6 flat shader or other small brush, paint around the shapes you have drawn and fill in the background. Paint a circular ring within the satellite shapes.

4
Outline the shapes with black permanent marker. Add details like spirals and small circles to the satellite shapes. Add black doodles over the glaze in a random pattern. Varnish to protect your work.

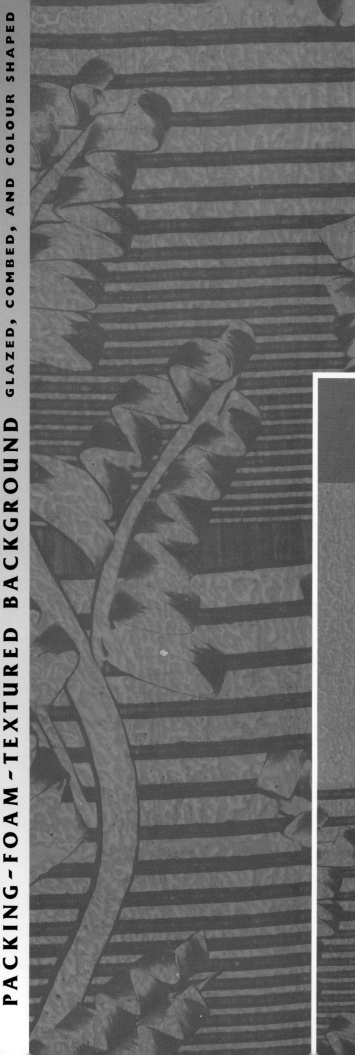

Here we go again, rummaging through the trash for art materials. This time the texturing tool is a sheet of thin (approximately one sixteenth of an inch) flexible packing foam. The tiny air bubbles in the foam create the texture.

To create this pattern, you will need:

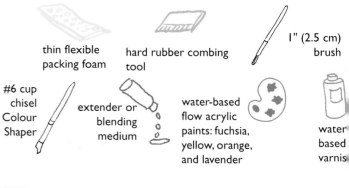

thin flexible packing foam

hard rubber combing tool

1" (2.5 cm) brush

#6 cup chisel Colour Shaper

extender or blending medium

water-based flow acrylic paints: fuchsia, yellow, orange, and lavender

water based varnis

1 Use the 1" (2.5 cm) brush to apply a base coat to the surface with fuchsia paint. Apply two coats of varnish. Allow the varnish to dry thoroughly.

2 Cut a piece of packing foam to suit your project. If the surface is small, you can texture all at once. If not, work a section at a time. Prepare a yellow-green glaze by mixing one part paint with one part water. Use the 1" (2.5 cm) brush to apply an even coat of glaze.

3 While the glaze is still wet, place the foam on top of the surface and press down evenly until it sticks to the surface. Peel the foam off. Blot the foam on paper towel or newspaper before glazing and texturing the next section. When you have finished texturing, apply two coats of varnish.

4 Prepare a lavender glaze by mixing one part paint with one part water. Use the 1" (2.5 cm) brush to apply an even coat of glaze over the textured and varnished surface, again working a section at a time. Use the hard rubber combing tool to form a horizontal grill. Then working quickly, use the #6 cup chisel Colour Shaper to incise a vine and leaf pattern into the combed texture. Varnish to protect your work.

he basic texture for this pattern is identical to the previous ttern. A dark glaze and a random, more abstract, pattern eate a brand new effect.

To create this pattern, you will need:

thin flexible
packing foam

1" (2.5 cm)
brush

#6 cup
chisel
Colour
Shaper

extender
or blending
medium

hard rubber
combing tool

water-based
flow acrylic
paints: fuchsia,
yellow-green,
and purple

water-based
varnish

Use the 1" (2.5 cm) brush to apply a base coat to the
surface with fuchsia paint. Apply two coats of varnish.
Allow the varnish to dry thoroughly.

Cut a piece of packing foam to fit your project. If the
surface is small, you can texture all at once. If not, work
a section at a time. Prepare a yellow-green glaze by
mixing one part paint with one part water. Use the 1"
(2.5 cm) brush to apply an even coat of glaze.

While the glaze is still wet, place the foam on top
of the surface and press down evenly until it sticks
to the surface. Peel the foam off. Blot the foam
on paper towel or newspaper before glazing and
texturing the next section. When you have
finished texturing, apply two coats of varnish.

Prepare a purple glaze by mixing one part paint with one
part water. Use the 1" (2.5 cm) brush to apply an even coat
of glaze over the textured and varnished surface, again
working a section at a time. Use the hard rubber combing
tool to form random thin and broad rectangular shapes.
Then working quickly, use the #6 cup chisel Colour Shaper
to incise an abstract tree pattern, sometimes overlapping
the combed texture. Varnish to protect your work.

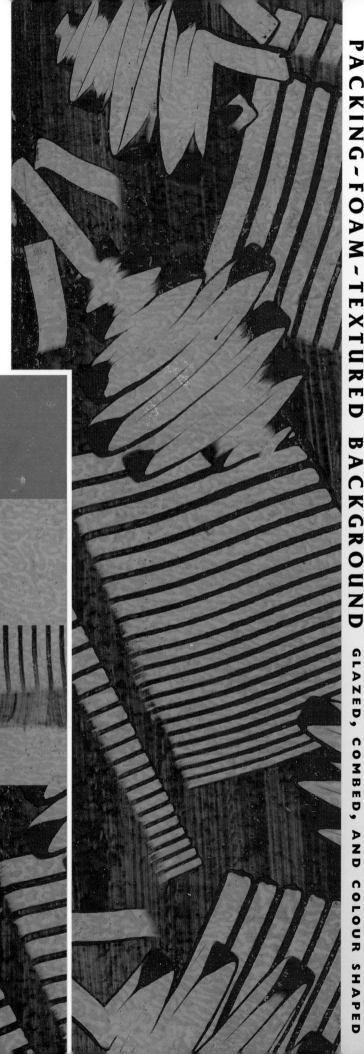

A common household product, plastic wrap, becomes a stamping tool to form one of five layers of paint and glaze. These layers build depth and create rich but subtle colors behind the combing and Colour Shaping incised into the top blue glaze.

To create this pattern, you will need:

clear plastic wrap

hard rubber combing tool

1" (2.5 cm) brush; #6 and #12 flat shaders

#6 cup chisel Colour Shaper

extender or blending medium

water-based flow acrylic paints: citrus yellow, lavender, coral, terra cotta, mauve, and blue

water-based varnish

Use the 1" (2.5 cm) brush to apply a citrus yellow base coat. Then add random confetti-like squares by painting short lavender strokes with the 1" (2.5 cm) brush, short coral strokes with the #12 flat shader, and slightly curved short terra cotta strokes with the #6 flat shader.

Prepare a mauve glaze by mixing one part paint with one part water. Cut a piece of plastic wrap about 12" (30 cm) long. Use the 1" (2.5 cm) brush to apply an even coat of glaze. Lay the plastic wrap on the glazed surface and press it together to wrinkle the plastic wrap, trapping glaze in the wrinkles. You will see the texture forming. Peel the plastic wrap off carefully.

When the textured surface is thoroughly dry, apply two coats of varnish. Prepare a blue glaze by mixing one part paint with one part water. When the varnish is dry, use the 1" (2.5 cm) brush to apply an even coat of glaze.

Use the hard rubber comb in a firm, but sweeping motion to form broad combed arcs. Working quickly, use the #6 cup chisel Colour Shaper to incise long and short, straight and curved lines to form a calligraphic pattern. Varnish to protect your work.

A rubber stamp removes glaze to allow the foam textured background to show through. This is called the "subtraction method." Color is taken away rather than added, forming a second texture. Then a top glaze is painted around the shapes, resulting in a bold pattern.

To create this pattern, you will need:

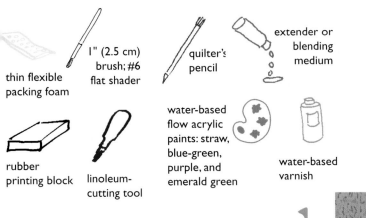

thin flexible packing foam

1" (2.5 cm) brush; #6 flat shader

quilter's pencil

extender or blending medium

rubber printing block

linoleum-cutting tool

water-based flow acrylic paints: straw, blue-green, purple, and emerald green

water-based varnish

1 Use the 1" (2.5 cm) brush to apply a base coat to the surface with straw paint. Apply two coats of varnish. Allow the varnish to dry thoroughly.

2 Cut a piece of packing foam to suit your project. If the surface is small, you can texture it all at once. If not, work a section at a time. Prepare a blue-green glaze by mixing one part paint with one part water. Use the 1" (2.5 cm) brush to apply an even coat of glaze.

3 While the glaze is still wet, place the foam on top of the surface and press down evenly until it sticks to the surface. Peel the foam off. Blot the foam on paper towel or newspaper before glazing and texturing the next section. When you have finished texturing, apply two coats of varnish.

4 Draw a design onto a block of rubber cut to the desired size. Then use the linoleum-cutting tool to incise the design. Be conservative in removing the rubber, remembering that what you leave forms the printing surface.

5 Keeping the stamp handy, prepare a purple glaze by mixing one part paint with one part water. Use the 1" (2.5 cm) brush to apply an even coat of glaze to the surface. Press the stamp into the glaze to remove glaze and begin the stamped pattern. Blot the stamp thoroughly and repeat another stamp. Apply a coat of varnish to seal your work.

6 Use a quilter's pencil to sketch straight and wavy lines and donut shapes over the textured surface. Prepare an emerald green glaze by mixing one part paint with one part water. Use the #6 flat shader brush to outline the shapes you have drawn and then fill in the background. Varnish to protect your work.

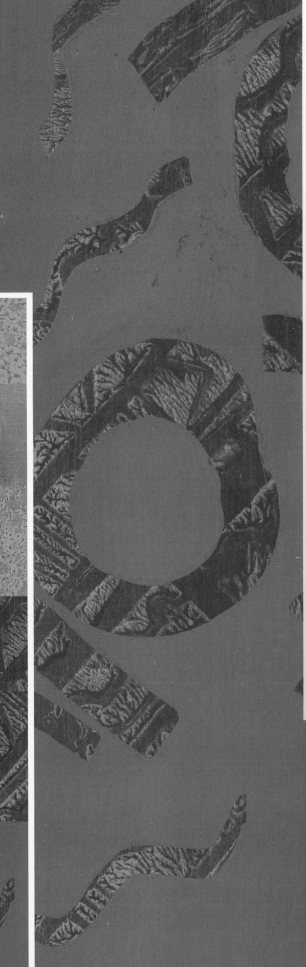

A hard rubber combing tool, used in short diagonal strokes from left to right and then from right to left, forms a herringbone lattice. The underlying texture created with large-holed rug liner shows through the lattice.

To create this pattern, you will need:

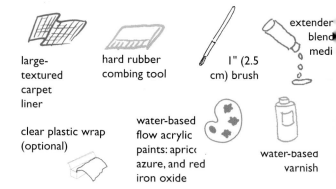

large-textured carpet liner

hard rubber combing tool

1" (2.5 cm) brush

extender blend medi

clear plastic wrap (optional)

water-based flow acrylic paints: apricot azure, and red iron oxide

water-based varnish

1 Use the 1" (2.5 cm) brush to apply an apricot base coat. Then apply two coats of varnish. Cut a piece of carpet liner to suit your needs.

2 Prepare an azure glaze by mixing one part paint with one part water. Use the 1" (2.5 cm) brush to apply an even coat of glaze. Apply the glaze to the surface with a broad brush. If the surface is large, work in sections.

3 Press the carpet liner smoothly and evenly into the wet glaze. If paint on your hands bothers you, you may wish to place a layer of plastic film over the carpet liner before applying pressure. Peel off the carpet liner. Apply two coats of varnish.

4 Prepare a red iron oxide glaze by mixing one part paint with one part water. Use the 1" (2.5 cm) brush to apply an even coat of glaze. Use the hard rubber combing tool and, moving from left to right in a diagonal direction, form short rectangles. Then turn the comb and move from right to left in the opposite diagonal direction to form the herringbone lattice. Varnish to protect your work.

What a difference color makes! The pattern on the facing page is almost identical to this one, except for a slight variation in the combing technique. A different palette results in a less pronounced texture that nonetheless forms a brilliant contrast to the light green lattice.

To create this pattern, you will need:

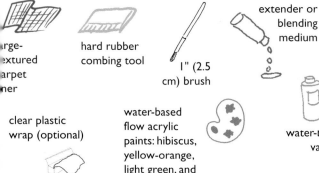

large-textured carpet liner

hard rubber combing tool

1" (2.5 cm) brush

extender or blending medium

clear plastic wrap (optional)

water-based flow acrylic paints: hibiscus, yellow-orange, light green, and red iron oxide

water-based varnish

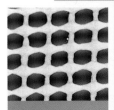

Use the 1" (2.5 cm) brush to apply a hibiscus base coat. Then apply two coats of varnish. Cut a piece of carpet liner to suit your needs.

Prepare a yellow-orange glaze by mixing one part paint with one part water. Use the 1" (2.5 cm) brush to apply an even coat of glaze. Apply the glaze to the surface with a broad brush. If the surface is large, work in sections.

Press the carpet liner smoothly and evenly into the wet glaze. If paint on your hands bothers you, you may wish to place a layer of plastic film over the carpet liner before applying pressure. Peel off the carpet liner. Apply two coats of varnish.

Prepare a light green glaze by mixing one part paint with one part water. Use the 1" (2.5 cm) brush to apply an even coat of glaze. Use the hard rubber combing tool and, moving from right to left in a diagonal direction, form broad rectangles. Then turn the comb and move from left to right in the opposite diagonal direction to form narrow rectangles. Varnish to protect your work.

Five different stamps in varying shapes, sizes, designs, and colors create a lively and interesting pattern. This pattern peeks through a blue glaze curtain, defined by the Colour Shaper.

To create this pattern, you will need:

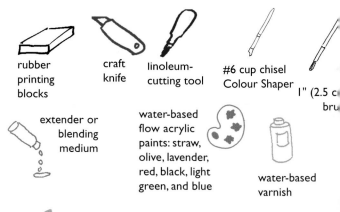

rubber printing blocks

craft knife

linoleum-cutting tool

#6 cup chisel Colour Shaper

1" (2.5 cm) brush

extender or blending medium

water-based flow acrylic paints: straw, olive, lavender, red, black, light green, and blue

water-based varnish

1 Use the 1" (2.5 cm) brush to apply a straw base coat. Cut the rubber block into five different sizes and shapes with a craft knife. Draw a design on each block with pencil. Then use the linoleum-cutting tool to incise the design. Be conservative in removing the rubber, remembering that what you leave forms the printing surface.

2 Use a 1" (2.5 cm) brush to apply a thin layer of olive paint to the largest stamp. Test the stamp on paper. If the design is clear, you are ready to proceed by repainting the block and stamping the fabric according to the design. Be careful not to get paint in the carved out lines. If you do, get rid of it with a clean brush. Test the other stamps in the same way.

3 Begin the pattern by applying olive paint and pressing the stamp firmly and evenly onto the surface to transfer the paint. Remove the stamp by lifting straight up. Reapply paint and continue stamping, leaving space between.

4 Continue in the same manner with red, black, lavender, and light green stamps. Allow stamps to overlap, but make sure the paint from the earlier stamps is dry before stamping over them.

5 When the paint from all the stamps is dry, apply two coats of varnish. Prepare a blue glaze by mixing one part paint with one part water. Use the 1" (2.5 cm) brush to apply an even coat of glaze. If the piece is large, work one section at a time. Use the #6 cup chisel Shaper to incise vertical wavy lines. Varnish to protect your work.

This pattern is similar to the pattern on the facing page except for the number of stamps, the palette, and the color shaped design. As you can see, a round tip Colour Shaper produces a markedly different line from the cup chisel shaper used in other patterns.

To create this pattern, you will need:

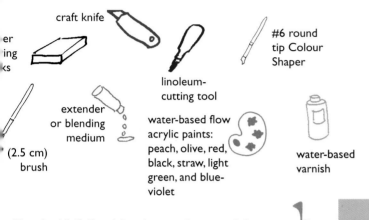

craft knife

#6 round tip Colour Shaper

linoleum-cutting tool

...er ...ing ...ks

extender or blending medium

water-based flow acrylic paints: peach, olive, red, black, straw, light green, and blue-violet

water-based varnish

(2.5 cm) brush

1 Use the 1" (2.5 cm) brush to apply a peach base coat. Cut the rubber block into six different sizes and shapes with a craft knife. Draw a design on each block with pencil. Then use the linoleum-cutting tool to incise the design. Be conservative in removing the rubber, remembering that what you leave forms the printing surface.

2 Use a 1" (2.5 cm) brush to apply a thin layer of olive paint to the largest stamp. Test the stamp on paper. If the design is clear, you are ready to proceed by repainting the block and stamping the surface according to the design. Be careful not to get paint in the carved out lines. If you do, get rid of it with a clean brush. Test the other stamps in the same way.

3 Begin the design by applying olive paint and pressing the stamp firmly and evenly onto the surface to transfer the paint. Remove the stamp by lifting straight up. Reapply paint and continue stamping, leaving space between.

4 Continue in the same manner with red, black, straw, and light green stamps. Allow stamps to overlap, but make sure the paint from the earlier stamps is dry before stamping over them.

5 When the paint from all the stamps is dry, apply two coats of varnish. Prepare a blue-violet glaze by mixing one part paint with one part water. Use the 1" (2.5 cm) brush to apply an even coat of glaze. If the piece is large, work one section at a time. Use the #6 round tip Colour Shaper to incise vertical and horizontal tear drops. Note that the round end of the teardrop is the beginning of the stroke. Varnish to protect your work.

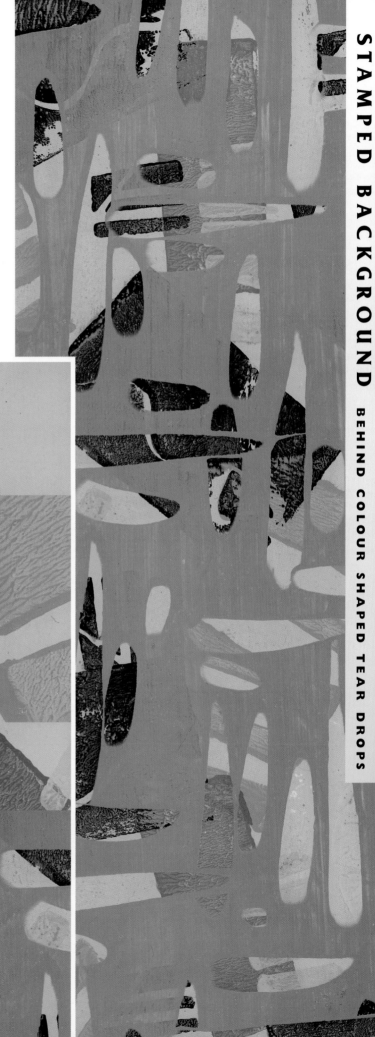

STAMPED BACKGROUND BEHIND COLOUR SHAPED TEAR DROPS

SPONGED AND STAMPED DESIGN WITH BLACK DOODLES

Sponges join hard rubber blocks as stamping tools. A permanent marking pen creates spirals, arches, and straight and zigzag lines.

To create this pattern, you will need:

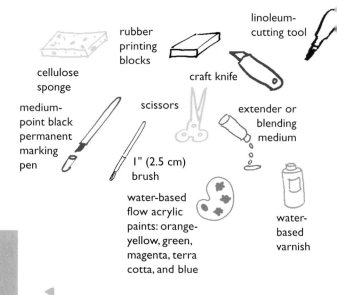

rubber printing blocks

linoleum-cutting tool

cellulose sponge

craft knife

medium-point black permanent marking pen

scissors

1" (2.5 cm) brush

extender or blending medium

water-based flow acrylic paints: orange-yellow, green, magenta, terra cotta, and blue

water-based varnish

1 Use the 1" (2.5 cm) brush to apply an orange-yellow base coat. Cut a cellulose sponge into a triangular shape and a donut shape. Apply blue paint to the triangle with the 1" (2.5 cm) brush. Press down gently to stamp the shape in a random pattern. Follow the same procedure to stamp terra cotta donut shapes.

2 Cut two small stamps from the rubber block with a craft knife. Draw a design on each block with pencil. Then use the linoleum-cutting tool to incise the design. Be conservative in removing the rubber, remembering that what you leave forms the printing surface.

3 Use a 1" (2.5 cm) brush to apply a thin layer of magenta paint to the square stamp. Press the stamp firmly and evenly onto the surface to transfer the paint. Remove the stamp by lifting straight up.

4 Test the stamp on paper. If the design is clear, you are ready to proceed by repainting the block and stamping a center in each terra cotta donut. Follow the same procedures to apply the green rectangular stamp.

5 When the paint from all the stamps is dry, use the black marker to create a free doodle-like design of spirals, arches, and straight and zigzag lines. Varnish to protect your work.

The pattern on the facing page shows through a pattern of combed arches. Other combed patterns call for a professional hard rubber comb. This time, the comb is homemade from ordinary household items.

To create this pattern, you will need:

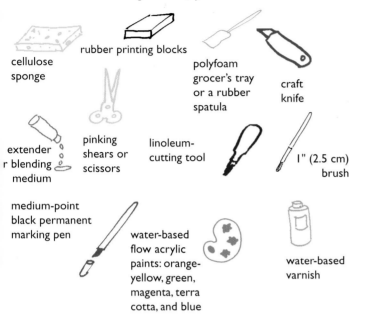

cellulose sponge

rubber printing blocks

polyfoam grocer's tray or a rubber spatula

craft knife

extender or blending medium

pinking shears or scissors

linoleum-cutting tool

1" (2.5 cm) brush

medium-point black permanent marking pen

water-based flow acrylic paints: orange-yellow, green, magenta, terra cotta, and blue

water-based varnish

1 Follow the steps on the facing page to create the background design. Apply two coats of varnish to form a slick surface.

2 Manufacture a simple combing tool by cutting a rubber kitchen spatula or 1" (2.5 cm) strip cut from a polyfoam grocer's tray. If you have pinking shears, cut straight across the spatula or polyfoam strip. Then cut the tips of the pinked edge away to form a crenelated edge. You can create the same effect with scissors alone.

3 Prepare a blue glaze by mixing one part paint with one part water. Use the 1" (2.5 cm) brush to apply an even coat of glaze. Apply your new combing tool in a curving motion to form rainbows. Varnish to protect your work.

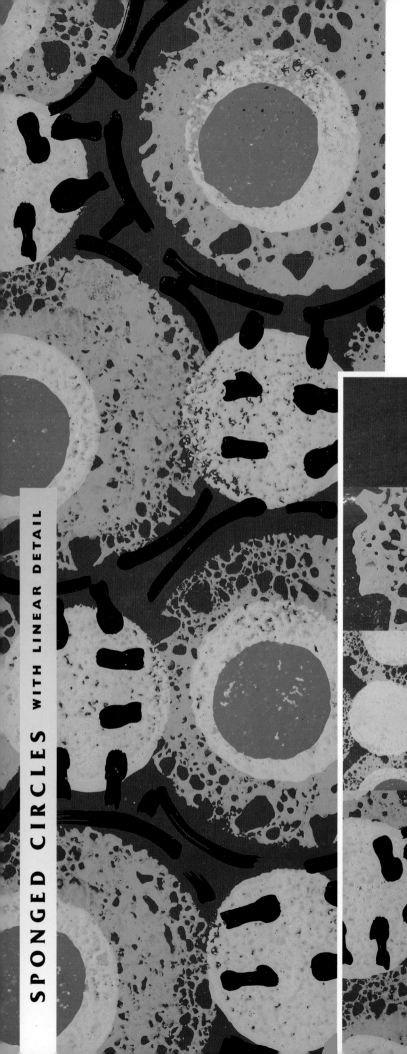

A kitchen sponge and household scissors become artists' tools to create this bold but simple pattern. The rich color contrasts and linear detail suggest an Art Deco influence.

To create this pattern, you will need:

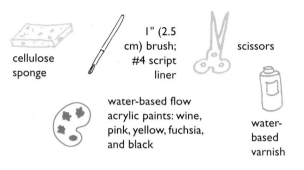

cellulose sponge

1" (2.5 cm) brush; #4 script liner

scissors

water-based flow acrylic paints: wine, pink, yellow, fuchsia, and black

water-based varnish

1 Use the 1" (2.5 cm) brush to apply a wine base coat. If you feel confident in your ability to stamp with sponges you can proceed directly to the next step. If you feel you may need to correct your work, apply two coats of varnish to provide a sealed base. This will allow you to correct mistakes with a damp paper towel.

2 Use the scissors to cut the sponge into three circles: one about 3" (7.5 cm), a second about 1 ³/₄ " (4.2 cm), and a third about 1" (2.5 cm) in diameter. Apply pink paint to the largest stamp. Blot slightly on paper towel or newsprint to remove excess paint. Then press down gently onto the base-coated surface.

3 Continue printing pink circles in a row, leaving an inch or so between each edge. Print the next row in a "half-drop" layout. That is, so that the circles in the second row fall between the circles in the first row.

4 Apply yellow paint to the mid-size sponge. Print a center for each pink circle and the same shape in the spaces between the pink circles. Next, apply fuchsia paint to the smallest circular sponges and print centers in the pink and yellow concentric circles.

5 Use the #4 script liner to outline the pink circles with black curved lines and irregular dashes. Create more interesting and varied lines by applying pressure at the beginning and ending of brushstrokes. Varnish to protect your work.

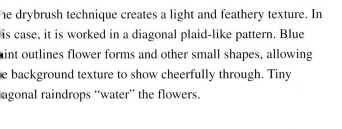

he drybrush technique creates a light and feathery texture. In
is case, it is worked in a diagonal plaid-like pattern. Blue
aint outlines flower forms and other small shapes, allowing
e background texture to show cheerfully through. Tiny
agonal raindrops "water" the flowers.

To create this pattern, you will need:

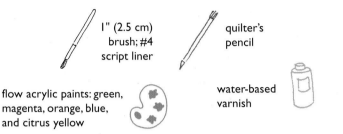

1" (2.5 cm)
brush; #4
script liner

quilter's
pencil

flow acrylic paints: green,
magenta, orange, blue,
and citrus yellow

water-based
varnish

1 The drybrush technique allows you to create a light,
textured stroke. To drybrush, dip the 1" (2.5 cm) brush in
orange paint. Then remove most of the paint, either by
squeezing with your fingers (the messy way) or by
wiping on paper towel or newsprint until the bristles of
the brush begin to spread slightly.

2 Using the drybrush technique and orange paint, apply
diagonal rows of short rectangles first in one direction,
then in the other. Apply sparingly, allowing for the
application of other colors. Repeat by drybrushing with
green and magenta paint. Leave plenty of paper showing.

3 Use the quilter's pencil to outline flowers, curves,
and other irregular shapes. With the #4 script liner
and blue paint, outline the shapes you have drawn,
then fill in the background.

4 Paint small blue centers in the flowers. Use the brush or
the wooden end of the script liner to add small dots to
form the flower pistils.

5 Use the #4 script liner and citrus yellow paint to create
diagonal rows of raindrops over the blue background.
Varnish to protect your work.

Simple painted shapes and a small stamp create the uncomplicated backdrop for an overlying combed pattern. Easy to execute steps produce a sophisticated result.

To create this pattern, you will need:

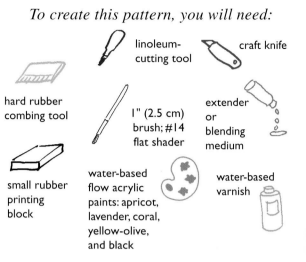

linoleum-cutting tool

craft knife

hard rubber combing tool

1" (2.5 cm) brush; #14 flat shader

extender or blending medium

small rubber printing block

water-based flow acrylic paints: apricot, lavender, coral, yellow-olive, and black

water-based varnish

1 Use the 1" (2.5 cm) brush to paint large lavender circles and horizontal and vertical rectangles. Although painting these large forms freehand is not difficult, you may wish to indicate their location with a quilter's pencil before painting.

2 Use the craft knife to cut a small stamp about 1" x 1" (2.5 cm x 2.5 cm). Use the linoleum-cutting tool to incise a simple linear design. Use the 1" (2.5 cm) brush to put black paint on the stamp. Press down firmly to apply paint. Stamp this design on the four quadrants of the large lavender circles and adjacent to some of the rectangles.

3 Use the #14 flat shader to paint small coral squares on either side of the stamped designs. Apply two coats of varnish.

4 Prepare a yellow-olive glaze by mixing one part paint with one part water. Use the 1" (2.5 cm) brush to apply an even coat of glaze. If you are covering a large surface, work one section at a time. Use the hard rubber comb to complete the pattern: a) Comb a vertical stripe, b) over-comb horizontal rectangles slightly to the right of the vertical stripe, then c) comb a vertical zigzag stripe to the right of the rectangles. Varnish to protect your work.

Simple painted elements create a bold pattern behind a combed texture. Note that this pattern is simultaneously very similar to and very different from the pattern on the facing page.

To create this pattern, you will need:

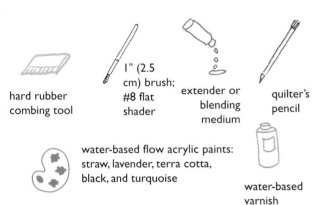

hard rubber combing tool

1" (2.5 cm) brush; #8 flat shader

extender or blending medium

quilter's pencil

water-based flow acrylic paints: straw, lavender, terra cotta, black, and turquoise

water-based varnish

Use the 1" (2.5 cm) brush to apply a straw base coat. Use the quilter's pencil to sketch in the diamond pattern near the top and middle of the pattern and a 2" (5 cm) stripe near the bottom.

Use the 1" (2.5 cm) brush and lavender paint to fill in the diamond band and the 2" (5 cm) band. Use the #8 flat shader to paint black zigzag lines parallel to the edge of the lavender zigzags.

Use the 1" (2.5 cm) brush and terra cotta paint to create large circles in the center of each lavender diamond. Then, with the same brush and paint color, add a checkerboard pattern to the lower straw and lavender stripes. Apply two coats of varnish.

Prepare a turquoise glaze by mixing one part paint with one part water. Use 1" (2.5 cm) brush to apply an even coat of glaze. If you are covering a large surface, work one section at a time. Use the hard rubber comb to complete the pattern: a) Comb a vertical stripe, then b) comb a vertical zigzag stripe to the right of the vertical stripe. Varnish to protect your work.

RESOURCES FOR THE DECORATIVE PAINTER

Most of the supplies for the projects shown can be found at your local art supply store. The following materials were used in the production of the decorative painting items demonstrated in this book. We have made every effort to ensure that names, addresses, and phone numbers are correct as of publication time.

PAINTS AND VARNISHES

Delta Ceramcoat flow acrylic paints and varnishes can be found in most art and craft stores. You can obtain color sheets, color conversion charts, and project sheets by sending a stamped, self-addressed envelope with your request, marked "Literature Request," to

Delta Technical Coating
2550 Pellissier Place
Whittier, CA 90601-1505

Other companies that produce high-quality paints include Americana, Liquitex, Folkart, and Accent.

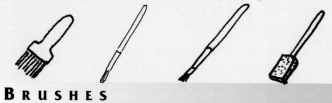

BRUSHES

Loew-Cornell will send a brush guide describing types of brushes and their uses if you send a stamped, self-addressed envelope with your request to:

Loew-Cornell
563 Chestnut Avenue
Teaneck, NJ 07666-2490

Other companies that produce high-quality brushes include Grumbacher, Liquitex, and Winsor & Newton.

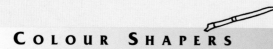

COLOUR SHAPERS

Forsline & Starr will send a booklet describing the types and sizes of Colour Shapers and their uses if you send a stamped, self-addressed envelope with your request to:

U.S. only:	U.K. and International:
Oasis America	Forsline & Starr, International
P.O. Box A	P.O. Box 76
Belle Mead, NJ 08502	Ware, Herts
	SG12 OYL England

RETAIL AND MAIL ORDER RESOURCES

Pearl Art and Craft retail stores carry a full array of products for the decorative painter. They are located in New York City and East Meadow, N.Y.; Miami, Ft. Lauderdale, Altamonte, and Tampa, Fla.; Atlanta, Ga.; Alexandria, Va.; Rockville, Md.; Paramus, Woodbridge, and Cherry Hill, N.J.; Cambridge, Mass.; Houston, Tex.; Chicago, Ill.; Philadelphia, Pa.; San Francisco and Los Angeles, Calif. You can obtain a catalog by calling: 800-221-6845.

Michael's is a chain of retail arts and craft stores throughout the United States, Puerto Rico, and Canada. To find the nearest store, call 972-409-1300, or write to them at 8000 Bent Branch Drive, Irving, Texas 75063.

Books and materials may be ordered from the Stan Brown Arts and Crafts catalog. To request a catalog, write to them at 13435 N.E. Whitaker Way, Portland, OR or call: (local Oregon) 503-252-9508; toll-free: 800-547-5531. There is a $5 charge for the catalog.

Supplies, including the double-primed floor cloth canvas used in the textiles section, may be ordered from Gregory D. Dorrance Co., 1063 Oak Hill Ave., Attleboro, MA 02703-7318. Phone: 508-222-6255; Fax: 508-222-6648.

SELECTED REFERENCES

Most large book stores stock an ample array of books of interest to the decorative painter, as do many arts and crafts stores. Most museums also carry art-related books in their retail shops. Here is a short list of books we have found especially helpful.

HISTORICAL PERSPECTIVE

de Dampierre, Florence. *The Best of Painted Furniture.* Rizzoli International, 1987

Fales, Dean A. *American Painted Furniture, 1660-1880.* Crown Publishers, 1988

Innes, Jocasta. *Scandinavian Painted Furniture.* Cassell, 1990

STYLE BOOKS

Jones, Owen. *The Grammar of Ornament.* Dover Publications, 1987

Jones, Owen. *The Complete Chinese Ornament.* Dover Publications, 1990

Verneul, M.P., et. al., Charles Rahn Fry, ed. *Art Nouveau Floral Ornament in Color.* Dover Publications, 1976

TECHNIQUES

Andre, Lee and David Lipe. *Decorative Painting for the Home.* Lark Books, 1995

Bell, Cressida. *The Decorative Painter.* Bulfinch Press, 1996

Wilhilde, Elizabeth, ed. *The Encyclopedia of Decorative Painting Techniques.* Running Press, 1994

Drucker, Mindy and Nancy Rosen. *More Recipes for Surfaces.* Simon & Schuster, 1995

Innis, Jocasta. *The New Paint Magic.* Pantheon Books, 1992

Jones, Andy. *Decorative Paint Finishes for the Home: A Complete Guide to Decorative Paint Finishes.* Watson-Guptill, 1996

Shaw, Jackie. *The Big Book of Decorative Painting.* Watson-Guptill, 1994

Wagstaff, Liz. *Paint Recipes: A Step-by-Step Guide to Colors and Finishes for the Home.* Chronicle Books, 1996

Walton, Stewart and Sall Walton. *Stamp Magic: Inspired Effects with the Easiest New Decorating Technique.* Lorenze Books, 1995

INDEX